30 Essential Typefaces for a Lifetime

ROCKPORT

First published in Taiwan ROC in 2006 by
Long Sea International Book Co., Ltd.
No.204 Si Wei Raod
Taipei 106 TAIWAN R.O.C.
Telephone: 886-2-2706-6838
Fax: 886-2-2-706-6109

First published in the United States of
America by Rockport Publishers, a member
of Quayside Publishing Group
33 Commercial Street
Gloucester, Massachusetts 01930-5089
Telephone: (978) 282-9590
Fax: (978) 283-2742
www.rockpub.com

Through the Rights and Production
arrangement by Rico Komanoya, ricorico,
Tokyo, Japan

ISBN 1-59253-278-0   347132

10 9 8 7 6 5 4 3 2 1

Design and Production: Pao & Paws, Taiwan
Associate Editor: Allison Dubinsky

Printed in China

30 Essential Typefaces for a Lifetime

Edited and curated by Imin Pao and Joshua Berger

Contents

Introduction

No matter what language you speak, the characters of that language were among the first things you learned. Letters are the signs and signifiers that we use to create meaning and to communicate. They tell stories and convey news. They sell products. They announce marriages. They record births and deaths. They tell you how to save a life or how to bake a cake.

But there's more to a letter than simply its sound or shape. The specific appearance of each character affects how we interpret the words we read. A phrase printed in an elegant script evokes a different response in the reader than the same words printed in a bold sans serif face, capital letters. The typeface that you might use to announce the birth of your daughter is most likely not the typeface you'd use to announce an upcoming yard sale, or the opening of a new neighborhood café. Then again, maybe it is…

Before the age of digital typography, most typefaces were designed for very specific clients and purposes. Yet as these typefaces have been made digitally available over the past twenty years, their histories are often overlooked or forgotten, the characters dislodged from their original context. They're used in new ways, for new purposes, and by anyone who would like to add them to his or her personal font arsenal, whether professional designer or casual typeface enthusiast.

As with anything in use over time, fonts must evolve to continue to be functional; and evolve they do, as designers modify the letterforms from era to era, subtly adjusting the characters to align them with changes in methods of viewing and reproduction. What looks good coming off a Vandercook letterpress may not look quite as good on a Flash website.

And then there's the matter of choice. Today a designer has thousands of typefaces available to choose from – all accessible online, within minutes, from anywhere in the world. With such a dizzying variety of options, it can be challenging to assess the strengths and weaknesses of each one, let alone to determine which would be best for the project at hand.

We felt it was time for a thorough assessment of the most functional typefaces in use today, taking into account their origins as well as examples of present-day use. After querying design department chairs at Rhode Island School of Design, California's Art Center College of Design, Yale University School of Art, Basel School of Design, and London's Central Saint Martins College of Art and Design, we arrived at the thirty typefaces collected here – an assortment that may or may not surprise you, but will, we hope, inspire you. Several of the designers and educators we quizzed generously contributed their own thoughts on particular typefaces, which we have collected here into two groups of essays: "Living with Type" and "Evolution of Type."

What are we saying when we select a font? Is it a pure expression of our aesthetic preferences? How much is this choice influenced by the conventions of our surroundings? And how much is informed by a knowledge and history of the typeface itself?

We hope this book will prove to be a valuable resource for designers at any stage of their career – students, practicing professionals, teachers of the trade – as they consider these questions. We hope that it will spark or satiate the curiosity of anyone with even a passing interest in the typography that surrounds him every day.

In an era when fonts go in and out of style in months, not years, these thirty typefaces have stood the test of time. Welcome to *30 Essential Typefaces for a Lifetime*.
– The Editors

Essays

Living with Type

Don't Try This at Home!

Cyrus Highsmith

Rhode Island School of Design

A typeface that I can't live without – this is what the publishers of this book asked me to write about. When I read their proposal, I had to ask myself: Do you need type to live? You need food to live. Also water. And things like oxygen. But do you need fonts to survive?

This is just the kind of question I have to tackle on a daily basis. I am a type designer at Font Bureau. Dealing with type is my full-time occupation – and then some. I decided to set up an experiment: Choose a typeface, completely eliminate it from my visual diet for twenty-four hours, and record the effects.

But please remember, I am a professional. For safety's sake, I had assistants standing by at all times in case a typographic emergency occurred and my life was threatened. Obviously, since I am writing this essay that you are now reading, I survived. I learned that it is possible to live without certain typefaces. But it was not easy, as you will see.

The first step of the experiment was to choose a typeface. I thought about choosing one of my favorite typefaces like Banco by Roger Excoffon. But Banco is not a typeface you see very often. That would make the experiment too easy. Therefore I made a list of some of the more popular typefaces. The kinds of fonts you see every day. At the top of the list were two clear candidates: Times New Roman and Helvetica. I flipped a coin. Helvetica won.

Helvetica was born not as Helvetica but as Neue Haas Grotesk. It was developed in 1957 by Edouard Hoffman, the director of the Haas Type Foundry in Switzerland. Max Miedinger made the drawings for it under the director's watchful eye. Hoffman also oversaw the development of other classics such as Clarendon, but Neue Haas Grotesk was his masterpiece.

In the mid-'60s the series was introduced in the United States by Mergenthaler Linotype thanks to their design director, Mike Parker. The American market was crazy for the new Swiss style of letter drawing, in which, according to Parker, "You draw the counters and let the black fall where it will."

In order to work on Linotype's machines, some alterations had to be made to the original Haas drawings. The italic was widened and the bold was narrowed so they fit on the same widths as the regular. Parker hated to do it. He felt the original designs from Haas were superior, but he had no choice. However, it is due in large part to the fact that Helvetica was distributed by Linotype that it became as successful as it did in the long run. It is these altered versions that still survive today in digital form.

Helvetica has easily been the world's most popular sans serif for some forty years. Today it is also arguably the world's most popular typeface of all. Its only rival is Times New Roman, a serif. These days almost anyone who has a laser printer can spit out a sign or a menu or whatever set in Helvetica. If you don't have a laser printer, you can buy it in the form of vinyl stickers. Helvetica is everywhere.

What follows is my journal of what happened when I spent a day without it.

A Day Without Helvetica: An Experiment

07:50

Morning. Time to get up. I am excited – a Helvetica-free day! What will happen? Will I survive this typographic adventure?

07:55

This doesn't look good. Almost all my clothes have labels set in Helvetica to explain how to wash them. I have found a Helvetica-free T-shirt, socks, and underwear, but no pants yet. I work at home, so it might not be a problem, but I was planning to go into the city today for a meeting. Yes, I need pants.

08:10

Find pants with no Helvetica in them – a pair of army surplus fatigues. No washing instructions or any labels at all. Lucky for me.

08:32

Go to make tea but discover Helvetica on the label of the tea package. I skip my usual breakfast yogurt for same reason. Fortunately I find a bag of green tea from Japan with no trace of the Roman alphabet on it, let alone Helvetica. Also find some unlabeled fresh fruit to eat.

09:00

Breakfast is finished. Upon hearing I will be going into the city, my wife asks me to pick up a few things at the grocery store that we can't get here. I inform her that I'll do it, but probably I won't be able to – the items will surely come in packages covered with labels printed in Helvetica. She seems puzzled, so I tell her about this important experiment I'm doing. She still seems puzzled.

09:10

Bus schedule is printed in Helvetica. I have to ask my wife to read it aloud to me.

10:50

I try to pay cash for my bus ticket but Helvetica appears on the back of the new U.S. dollars. My choice is either to pay with many handfuls of coins that I don't have, or to find a Helvetica-free credit card. I'm happy to discover my Citibank card employs Interstate as the sans serif instead of Helvetica. I charge my ticket.

11:00

On board bus to the city. Fortunately it is a Helvetica-free vehicle. I almost bought a newspaper to read on the trip, but all of them are full of the typeface I am trying to avoid. The *New York Times* uses Helvetica in its charts and for the agate. The *Boston Globe* and the *Wall Street Journal* are Helvetica-free in the news but not in the advertisements. No newspaper for me today.

12:33

Arriving in the city. Most of the signage at the bus terminal is set in Frutiger, but for some reason a couple are set in Helvetica. I quickly duck to avoid those. Close call!

12:40

I try to catch the subway uptown so I can go to the comic-book store. But I run into trouble at the subway token machine. The instructions for how to buy a token are printed in Helvetica. So I start to buy a token from the person at the turnstile, only to realize that every sign in the station is printed in Helvetica. No subway for me today. I will stick to neighborhoods I can walk to.

13:15

I'm getting hungry – time for lunch. Remembering my luck at breakfast with Helvetica-free Asian packaging, I head for Chinatown. I arrive at my favorite noodle shop, but I have to turn away – the menu is printed in Helvetica.

13:55

Still looking for a Helvetica-free restaurant. The menus in the windows are full of it. Getting very hungry.

14:15

Success! I finally find a Vietnamese sandwich shop with handwritten menus posted on the walls. No Helvetica here. The sandwiches also turn out to be excellent.

15:00

Arrive at the office to check email and have my meeting. I previously deleted all versions of Helvetica from my hard drive just to be safe. Everyone at the meeting was screened for visible signs of Helvetica beforehand. So I am able to pass some relatively uneventful Helvetica-free hours.

20:20

Get home a bit late because I couldn't remember the bus schedule and I missed the first bus. I am very happy to discover my wife has decided to join me in the experiment. She has removed the label from a wine bottle so we can have a drink together. The label contained a warning set in Helvetica that cautioned us not to have too much to drink.

20:50

To avoid any food labeled with Helvetica, we decide to have just a salad and some potatoes for dinner. I am in charge of cleaning the potatoes. My wife handles any food that comes from a package. It occurs to me that without her there to handle packaged food, I might get very hungry. Or, at least, sick of potatoes very soon.

21:05

I offer to wash the dishes but discover the soap bottle has Helvetica on it. Another warning, this one about keeping the soap away from children. I guess I will do them in the morning when my Helvetica-free twenty-four hours are over.

21:10

Reading one of my favorite books – *The Long Goodbye* by Raymond Chandler. It is set in one of my favorite types, Electra. We had rented a video to watch, but I discovered the buttons on the television are labeled with Helvetica. Same with the stereo. So it is a quiet night.

22:20

Not that I mind spending a night of quiet reading. I enjoy it. But for a typeface that most designers describe as monotonous, Helvetica is rather ubiquitous. Your life can become boring without it; you run out of options mighty quick. Where's that bottle of wine without the label?

Conclusion:

I survived my twenty-four hours without Helvetica. But it wasn't easy. Everywhere you turn, you'll find this typeface. Helvetica explains how to take care of your clothes. It tells you when to catch the bus. It informs you about the food you eat. Helvetica warns you not to drink too much and protects our children from getting soap in their eyes. I like Helvetica for all the small tasks it carries out every day. Thanks to the lucky combination of the strength of its design and its excellent distribution, it has been incorporated into almost every detail of modern life. So next time you see Helvetica (which will be soon!), take a moment to ponder its place in the world and your life. There will never be another typeface like it.

Nutrition Facts

Serving Size 2 crackers (14 g)
Servings Per Container About 21

Amount Per Serving

Calories 60   Calories from Fat 15

	% Daily Value*
Total Fat 1.5g	**2%**
Saturated Fat 0g	**0%**
Polyunsaturated Fat 0g	
Monounsaturated Fat 0.5g	
Cholesterol 0mg	**0%**
Sodium 140mg	**6%**
Total Carbohydrate 10g	**3%**
Dietary Fiber Less than 1g	**3%**
Sugars 0g	
Protein 2g	

Vitamin A 0%	•	Vitamin C 0%
Calcium 0%	•	Iron 2%

* Percent Daily Values are based on a 2,000 calorie diet. Your daily values may be higher or lower depending on your calorie needs:

	Calories:	2,000	2,500
Total Fat	Less than	65g	80g
Sat Fat	Less than	20g	25g
Cholesterol	Less than	300mg	300mg
Sodium	Less than	2400mg	2400mg
Total Carbohydrate		300g	375g
Dietary Fiber		25g	30g

1

9659   S 60

MACHINE WASH WARM NORMAL
CYCLE. DO NOT BLEACH. TUMBLE
DRY HOT. HOT IRON IF NEEDED.
WASH AND DRY WITH LIKE COLORS.
COLOR MAY TRANSFER WHEN NEW.
WASH BEFORE WEARING.
WPL 423

680

501 0198 75719-5

00505 – 0260

2

M TRUCKING
06 TOMPKINS AV
K. N.Y 11216

3

1
The nutrition facts on almost all food packaging – at least in the United States – are printed in Helvetica.

2
Here, Helvetica appears on a pants label, explaining how to wash them.

3
Vinyl Helvetica stickers.

I Have Only One Typeface Which I Use and Love

Wolfgang Weingart

Basel School of Design

My work may well have been influenced by Serial Art, or by Repetition Typography practiced in the class of Emil Ruder during the '60s. The typeface Univers, designed by Adrian Frutiger of Switzerland, a longtime friend of Ruder, offered the Basel School a progressive approach to the arrangement of typography. The design of Univers was ideal for Ruder's own typographic work and that of his students. Hans-Rudolf Lutz, who studied at the Basel School for one year, from 1963 to 1964, especially favored it. Lutz and a few of his colleagues designed typographic pictures that would have been difficult to compose in any other typeface.

Univers was the first entire font system to be designed with interchangeable weights, proportions, and corresponding italics since the invention of book printing. In the design of older typefaces, visual alignment among such variations was not a standard consideration. For a given size of type all twenty-one variations of Univers, whether light, regular, medium, bold, condensed, expanded, or italic, had the same x-height (the height of lowercase letters without ascenders or descenders) and the same baseline. Letterpress printing simplified and increased the possibilities for visual contrast in tone, weight, width, and direction, making each typeface available in eleven sizes for metal typesetting.

When I came to the Basel School of Design, the coarse Berthold Akzidenz-Grotesk, so rarely used, was fast asleep in the type drawer under a blanket of dust. I woke it up.

Excerpted from *Weingart: My Way to Typography*, by *Wolfgang Weingart*. Lars Muller Publishers, 2001

Avenir

Henk van Assen

Yale University School of Art

At first I was surprised to find Avenir considered to be among the thirty "most useful and functional fonts in use today." Compared to many of the other fonts on the list, Avenir isn't used all that often. It is more common in Europe than in the United States. In fact, it was recently used in the design for the City of Amsterdam's visual identity.

In all honesty, my experience with Avenir hasn't been extensive. However, I clearly remember my first encounter with it, back in graduate school. I felt an immediate affinity with its visual appearance, in particular the medium and heavy forms. At first glance, I believed it to be a mix of the Futura and the Frutiger, so it wasn't surprising to learn that Adrian Frutiger had designed it. He had wanted to design a linear sans serif in the tradition of Erbar and Futura; he also aimed "to make use of the stylistic developments of the twentieth century." The font's name, *Avenir*, means "future" in French — so a semantic and conceptual connection with Futura also seems logical.

Futura's roots lie in the 1920s, when, during their tenure at the Bauhaus, Herbert Bayer and others explored the creation of constructed, purely geometrical letterforms, i.e. "Universal Type" (1925). In 1928, Paul Renner drew Futura. He made optical adjustments to the geometric letterforms in the areas where circles meet with vertical and horizontal lines. This helped increase Futura's legibility.

With Avenir, Frutiger has taken this concept further. Although its appearance has a strong geometric feeling, closer inspection reveals many subtle and unique nuances. The vertical strokes are thicker than the horizontals; the "o" is not a perfect circle; the upstrokes of the capitals "A," "K," "V," and "W" are thinner than the downstrokes; and the "a," "f," "r," and "t" have a more humanistic appearance than that of Futura or Avant Garde, another typeface with which Avenir is often compared. Furthermore, Avenir's ascenders are relatively short, which was done, Frutiger explained in an interview with Linotype Library, "on the well-established grounds that the human eye takes in horizontals more easily than verticals and tends to grasp the meaning of a line in a horizontal sweep."

Anyone familiar with Frutiger's other fonts (including Univers and Frutiger) will not find it difficult to recognize the regular and precise rhythm of the letters in Avenir, both in their forms and counterforms. As with other Frutiger fonts, Avenir does not use a true italic but is sloped at an angle of about twelve degrees.

One of the likely reasons that Avenir has not been used extensively is that, upon its release in 1988, only six basic weights — light (35), book (45), roman (55), medium (65), and the additional heavy (85) and black (95) — were available. Oddly enough, the bold (75) is not part of the collection. This limited selection of weights is quite remarkable from the man who designed Univers, which, with its diverse family and precise numbering system to distinguish among the many weights and variants, aimed for functionality and integration, and provided graphic designers with a wide array of possibilities to give text organization and visual expression.

What makes Avenir so attractive is its ability to be simultaneously rigorous, even perfectionist, and yet softer than the strict Univers and Frutiger typefaces. Univers is often accused of being "neutral" or "boring." Although I don't agree, I suspect that Avenir is in no danger of similar accusations. It is a highly personal, unique font that can be used in fine typography and advertising displays alike.

Thoughts Relating to the Typeface Univers

Simon Johnston

Art Center College of Design

Truth be told, I am not prepared to say that Univers is necessarily the most important typeface of all time, although it must certainly be in the top five contenders for that impossible label. However, I do think it has been one of the most significant contributions to typography in the twentieth century and represents a European cultural milestone – one of the flowerings of a modernist design sensibility whose roots lie in the radicalism and reductivism of Constructivism and the Bauhaus, allied to a later postwar sense of renewal – a true expression of the modern age.

Adrian Frutiger, a Swiss designer working in Paris, designed Univers in the 1950s. Released in 1956, it was the first typeface to be conceived as a related family of twenty-one fonts, and was also the first typeface to be manufactured simultaneously as hand-set metal type, monotype mechanical type, and photo type – bridging all the technological methods developed over the previous four centuries of typesetting. It featured an innovative numbering system for the different weights, with the 55 regular serving as the heart of the matrix from which other variations followed. The first digit refers to the weight, the second the slant. Roman is indicated by odd numbers, italics by even. Thus 73 is bold extended, while 48 is light condensed italic. It is in itself a beautifully crystalline organizational system, reflecting the purity and logic of the letterforms themselves.

The font was not originally called Univers. As Adrian Frutiger later recalled: "I liked the name Monde because of the simplicity of the sequence of letters. The name Europe was also discussed; but Charles Peignot (the typefounder who released the font) had international sales plans for the typeface and had to consider the effect of the name in other languages. Monde was unsuitable for German, in which der Mond means 'the moon.' I suggested 'Universal,' whereupon Peignot decided, in all modesty, that 'Univers' was the most all-embracing name!"

Some see the font as emotionally cool, and there may be some truth in this when it is compared with more recent humanistic sans fonts such as Thesis Sans, designed by Lucas de Groot, one of the masterpieces of recent digital font design. However, the forms of Univers are not merely utilitarian in a cold functional way, but possess a subtle, lyrical, humanistic quality as well, particularly in the lightest 45 weight.

I prefer to think of Univers as open or neutral, a quality that often comes up for discussion with students. In talking about neutrality with regards to a font, I am not using the term in a negative sense, but in the sense that the forms themselves are not overloaded with individualistic eccentricities or particular stylistic quirks that would render them usable for only a small number of situations. Imagine a sliding scale of typefaces with the two extremes of the scale being represented by neutrality/less fashion/utility/modesty at one end, and at the other end overt personality/high fashion/idiosyncratic form/low utility. Typefaces at the former end of the scale are those that could accommodate many different kinds of content; the shapes of the forms will not distract the reader from the content, or color the meaning of the text with their own formal expression. Univers would be here, along with the more generic Helvetica and even the utilitarian Courier. Typefaces at the latter end of the scale would have a very distinct personality – display fonts that would consequently limit their usage to the few situations where the evocative forms are appropriate expression for the content (add your own choices here: Shatter, Baby Teeth, Exocet, etc.).

"But, but, but," I hear some students say, "I need personality in my fonts – Univers is boring." This attitude usually comes from students, hipsters, and ironists thinking that typography is only about which font you choose rather than how you use the font ("I chose a cool font, therefore my design will be cool"). It also comes about because in the age of designers-promoted-as-celebrities, design students are apt to think that they are somehow artists and that self-expression is their mission and therefore expressive fonts are all that is needed. As designers we are messengers – we are not the message – and so it follows that fonts that serve language, that serve communication in a quiet, unfussy way, with a little humility, are more useful, and typography, ultimately, is about communicating. Of course it is also a form of expression – it cannot help being otherwise, as a byproduct of utility – but this is not its reason for being, as it is with fine art, where expression is freed from utility.

But typography is not just a matter of font choice. In the wrong hands even an excellent font such as Univers can be made to look like rubbish, whereas in the hands of a master the font becomes the agent for clarity and understanding; see the lucid crystalline compositions of Helmut Schmidt or the assured architectonic structures of Willi Kunz.

I sometimes wonder whether there is a correlation between the qualities of neutrality as perceived in the fonts Univers and Helvetica, and the historical political neutrality of Switzerland. Did the Swiss internalize this sense of neutrality? Could their need for official communication to be set in four languages (French, German, Italian, and Romansch), and the need for consensus have had an influence on the designers giving form to these letters? Could these conditions translate into a predilection for searching for universal forms? The idea of universal forms links to the idealistic notion of objective communication. Can there be such a thing? Perhaps only in a rationalist's dream.

One of the goals of the reductivist, high modernist, Swiss or International Style of typography was a desire to communicate in the clearest, most efficient and logical way possible, with no emphasis given to the personal tastes of the individual designer – the subjugation of the subjective in the quest for clarity and information. There is something both quixotic and Calvinist in this. But of course the desire to design with no apparent stylistic mannerisms is in itself an impossibility. No style is a style. The taste and choices of the designer will always be present.

More recently Frutiger was asked by the Linotype company to assist and advise on an enlarged, fully digitized version of the family, some forty-five years after the initial release of the font. The new version, Linotype Univers 3.0, released in 1997, features an expanded and refined range of fifty-nine fonts in total, with a graduated range of nine weights. Even the numbering system has been updated. Each font is designated by a three-digit number: the first digit designates weight, the second width, and the third slant. Therefore, 321 is light condensed italic, 940 is extra black extended roman, and 110 ultra light compressed roman. The increased weight range provides opportunities for subtle contrasts and nuanced emphasis not even possible with the original. The Univers is indeed expanding, just as the scientists tell us.

Modes and fashions occur in graphic design and typography just as they do in other areas of society. The pendulum swings from international style to historical pastiche to deconstructivist theory-lite to funky vernacular to retro modernism to digital baroque. Typically the speed with which a trend comes into style is equaled by the speed with which it disappears.

Fashion is exactly that which goes out of fashion. Univers seems almost to exist outside of these considerations – its qualities more fundamental and timeless – surveying the vicissitudes of passing fads with an assurance borne of nearly fifty years of use. A true classic. Though I have used the font, and my admiration for the achievement that is Univers remains undiminished, I now tend toward the slightly more personal qualities of Monotype Grotesque or the sympathetic humanist warmth of Thesis sans. But looking again at these newer Univers ultra-light weights…

Essays

Evolution of Type

Out of the Darkness

DIN and the Mythic Power of Type

Stanley Moss

Students of typographic design are forced to initially consider the technical issues of optical engineering for the visual universe. Yet they rarely focus on the ideological underpinnings and conundrums. The student of typography often views his or her subject as a series of rigid constraints, principles of scale and proportion and mechanical possibilities, fair game for manipulation. Rarely is typography viewed as part of an organic process of evolution, a working construct of ephemeral existence in a greater time continuum. As fonts evolve they carry forward echoes of the history that created them and the myths they bear. One cannot easily place a monetary value on myth, though some will try.

How deeply a brand values typography – and its ability to carry forward myth – varies widely. The little players use generic, esoteric, or readily available letters for their corporate signatures and communications. Some companies commission custom letterforms. Some eventually buy global licenses for entire typefaces, attaching their own myth or borrowing from that of the typeface. Some fonts, such as Times Roman, Fraktur, Playbill, Clarendon, and Old English migrated into mythical presences themselves.

Such a font is DIN, whose creation by Wagner in 1932 yielded a typographic institution so grandly proliferated as to be imitated to this day. We are awash in its grotesque children. As always, a window backwards serves to remind how and why.

The earliest monotone letterforms, composed of strokes of even thickness, can be traced to written ancient Greek from the fifth to second century B.C. From them comes the name "Grotesque," and the designation "sans serif." The casual baseline seen in fragments extant belies a letterform suited to the sparest elegance and economy, allowing lofty flights of random artistry. Later, the Romans, with their chisel serifs, drove the Grotesque into hiding for two thousand years. Letterforms approximated handwriting for centuries to follow, even to the dawn of moveable type. While the eventual introduction of serif fonts widely succeeded, it was not until 1816 that we can track the first recorded reappearance of a sans serif font in Germany, a transnational typeface that followed the Napoleonic era of plunder and destruction. The primary uses of the font were for display purposes, and there was little understanding of the interaction between individual characters. The elemental caps adhered to simplistic geometric modeling, with perfectly round counters, wider footing, the near-equilateral pyramid "A," a scenario of uncompromising kerning. This was a typeface that symbolized enlightenment coming from the face of darkness, with stoic freedom in all communications. It was a typeface heralding the industrial age with its relentless mechanical precision.

Around 1898, at the exact cultural moment when Art Nouveau was transitioning into an era of protofuturism, anticipating the emergence of Art Deco, two pivotal typefaces appeared. Akzidenz Grotesk was designed with an economic, verticality modeled on the demands of moveable metal or machine-set type, introducing an upward compression expressed in condensed letterforms, which were meant to be mechanically arrayed. Copperplate Condensed, of the same era, was produced no doubt to satisfy the demands of the cabal of serifim, but produced in an uppercase only. Copperplate's cap set roughly emulates that of Akzidenz, both in proportion and drafting, as well as in optical color. Neuzeit Grotesque, cut in 1928 by Wilhelm Pischner, adapted the thick regular strokes and square corners of Akzidenz, suggesting an even stricter rectangularity and harsher geometry. DIN, whose earliest incarnation dates from 1930, and its near relation, Umkerschrift, are Bauhaus-inspired in their affinity to form and function.

It was the decision of the German Standard Committee in 1936 that DIN 1451 be specifically employed in technology, traffic, administration, and business. The Committee deemed the type easily read and written, promoting its ubiquity. But there soon came vivid debate about the typeface's aesthetic attributes. Of course the artists won, and DIN quickly infected the artistic realm, insinuating itself into advertising with a singular vengeance. DIN's cap set was approximately modeled on the letterforms of Akzidenz, largely assuming the optical character and color of Copperplate Condensed. Curve stress of the counters is most apparent in the lowercase "a," "m," "n," and "r." DIN's numerals have been simplified and streamlined for the convenience of the end user. There is a loftiness in DIN's intent, which believes everything can work together, while things florid and artistic shall occupy their own space; DIN's rapid adoption for aesthetic uses refuted any such preposterous limitation.

The 1950s saw the emergence of highly evolved industrial fonts designed by enlightened and talented typographers: Univers, which celebrated the aesthetic of precision; and Helvetica, which promoted the mass proliferation of the mundane. Both made a lasting impression on communication, literacy, and taste. The essential impersonal blandness of Helvetica, though, came to symbolize a world homogenized, devoid of any humanistic refinement.

Thus in 1995 Albert-Jan Pool created the magnificent FF DIN, rebuilding this herald of the end of the industrial age with a grace, elegance, and ease superimposed on a matrix of formal, architectural right angles. This recutting created a standard of beauty and function, spawning a tidal wave of imitators all possessed of a cold and clinical mediocrity, which managed to obfuscate the mythical quality of the original. It is a curse of our era that dissolution and devaluation are often the result of high technology's ease of operation. Everyone can be a typographer, the mistaken idea goes. But the newer cuttings looked antiseptic, uninspired, over-refined to the point of the innocuous.

In 2002, adidas, a German athletic footwear company, commissioned a proprietary font family of twelve faces named adiHAUS, created to communicate the sensibilities of their brand. Plazm Fonts, retained for the project, proposed basing its earliest letterforms on a classic, antique cutting of Wagner's Umkerschrift.

The key word to remember with adidas is competition. While Nike built its brand on performance, adidas had attached itself primarily to professional competition and is credited with almost all athletic footwear innovations prior to Nike's waffle sole, which was introduced in the 1970s. Witness the recent resurgence of interest in classic adidas Olympic shoes from the 60s and 70s. The mythos of the brand is embedded in the concept. Plazm Font's project creative director Pete McCracken symbolically referenced this by introducing the typographic idea of setting oneself up in opposition to the past, drawing differences between the forerunner named DIN 1451 and the challenger named adiHAUS. Times had changed, too. The designers rendered adiHAUS more extended, more open in the counters, suggesting a more stable base, a more assured landing, and the foundations of balance. Paradoxically, the designers added a slightly higher waistline, rendering the font even more bottom-heavy with a lower center of gravity, an effect not mediated by a deeper descender line. AdiHAUS is a contrarian font where the lowercase "a," "i," and "y" stand simplified in symbolic opposition to their DIN antecedents, while the numerals "1" and "9" engage in a comparable conflict, only in reverse. AdiHAUS has altered the altitude of center horizontal strokes in "A," "B," "E," "F," "G," "P," and "R" to reflect the volumes of the extended counters – but other than that and some manipulation of the cap "Q," the uppercase is largely undistinguished, an homage to DIN, and a concession to our antipathy toward uppercase, which in the digital world is considered loud, pushy, and aggressive. Finally, adiHAUS demands and seizes more horizontal and vertical space proportionately than its predecessors, symbolizing the brand's attachment to the gains of competition. While the font met the objectives of the commercial mythos, it left behind the very mnemonic signals of its heritage.

Adidas eventually retired adiHAUS in 2004, instead opting for a global license of FF DIN from Font House, which administers world rights. We can only speculate on the true rationale, for the company had invested a year and a substantial sum to create their own proprietary typeface, then quickly abandoned it. In that action, adidas demonstrated how much and how little it valued typography. Perhaps the myth of FF DIN outshone the myth of adidas — so that the company sought to place less emphasis on competition, and more on coming out of the darkness and into the light.

There is a classic Zen koan that talks about what is outside the vessel being as important as the space within. AdiHAUS pushed adidas into the zone outside the vessel, and (to employ a student typographer's vocabulary) thereby redefined the meaning of the term "negative space."

As a footnote, Albert - Jan Pool writes:

"In 1905 the Prussian Railways were the first to define a model for lettering. Its original purpose was to unify the descriptions on freight cars. Soon it was adapted for all sorts of lettering, including the names of the railway stations.

The foundation of the Weimar Republic, which turned the patchwork of states into a single German state, was followed by a merger of all state railways into the Deutsche Reichsbahn in 1920. The master drawings of the Prussian Railways became the reference for all railway lettering.

During the Dessau Period of the Bauhaus, characters were drawn with ruler and compass on coarse grids. Doing so, Herbert Bayer and Joost Schmidt — who were responsible for the typographic courses — became exponents of the so-called Constructivist style of lettering. In the 1920s Constructivism was not the only game in town, but it certainly played an eminent role.

It is my personal guess that it was the Berthold foundry that was involved. Bernd Möllenstädt told me this some time ago, but within another context. The force behind the modelling of characters in the direction of Akzidenz Grotesk is said to be G. G. Lange, as well as Berthold. Lange had been a member of the DIN Committee of Drawings, and the later Committee of Type.

The work on DIN 1451 was supervised by Ludwig Goller, an employee of Siemens. With minor modifications the typeface of the Deutsche Reichsbahn (identical with that of one of its predecessors, the Prussian Railways) was turned into DIN Engschrift., which became the basic model for the signage version of DIN Mittelschrift and DIN Breitschrift. It seems that the company appreciated the work of its employee (also president of the DIN Committee of Drawings) so much that the characters of his newly drawn DIN Mittelschrift became the model for the new Siemens logotype from 1936 (Art Direction by Hans Domizlaff). As from the start of the development of DIN, which began around 1925, until the most recent versions of 1985, one main guideline forms the basis of all designs. Characters would be drawn with all kinds of tools, varying from drawing pens, engraving tools as well as compass and rulers. They all should share the same heartline. Depending on the tool, stroke ends could be rounded or angular. This is contradictory to all traditional forms of typography in which it is considered that only varying stroke weight enables optimal word-images.

Nevertheless there have been different versions of DIN from the very beginning. Not only was there the DIN typeface used for signage, of which the Adobe-Version DIN Mittelschrift and DIN Engschrift are the 'modern' versions. There was also a typeface for engraving (based on or identical with DIN 16 and 17), and also one for stencil lettering."

DIN

ABCDEFGJKLMNOPQURSTUVWXYZ
abcdefghijklmnopqurstuvwxyz
0123456789

adiHAUS

ABCDEFGJKLMNOPQURSTUVWXYZ
abcdefghijklmnopqurstuvwxyz
0123456789

JQZacdilry19

adiHAUS Regular

adiHAUS Bold

adiHAUS Bold Italic

adiHAUS Italic

adiHAUS Semi-Bold

adiHAUS Semi-Bold Italic

adiHAUS Condensed Regular

adiHAUS Condensed Bold

adiHAUS Condensed Italic

adiTECH Bold

2

Studio: Plazm
Creative Director: Pete
McCracken
Lead Designer: Gus Nicklos
Designers: Pete McCracken,
Gus Nicklos, Carole Ambauen,
Long Lam
Client: adidas

1
Alphabet specimen:
the adiHAUS typeface
in comparison to DIN.

2
The adiHAUS family.

The Making of Avenir Next

Akira Kobayashi

Linotype Library GmbH

My current role as a typeface director at Linotype Library GmbH is to plan and develop the new typeface collection for professional designers, which is named the Platinum Collection, and to design the typefaces for the collection. In the past three years, I have redesigned three well-known typefaces by collaboratively working with the original designers. Hermann Zapf and I redesigned Optima Nova and Zapfino Extra in 2003. In April 2004, Adrian Frutiger and I completed the redesign of Avenir Next, which was the first collaborative work we have done. Adrian is well known for designing sans serif typefaces such as Univers and Frutiger. In a typeface project such as the Platinum Collection, the type designer and the type foundry establish a new relationship that differs from the relationship they had in the times of letterpress printing and photocomposition. Today, it is possible to provide the users with better typefaces that reflect the essential beauty of the letters by giving a shape to the true intention of the original designer and expressing this without any physical limitations.

Avenir was first released from Linotype in 1988. Since then, Avenir had always been high on the best-selling list. According to Frutiger, Avenir was a geometric sans serif typeface "aiming for a better Futura." Futura met the standard of German typefaces in the early twentieth century. The letters "g," "j," "p," "q," and "y" of Futura had short descenders (the portions that extend below the baseline) compared to the long ascenders (the portions that extend above x-height) for the letters "b," "d," "f," "h," "k," and "l" giving the impression that the letters "g," "j," "p," "q," and "y" are extremely shrunken. Avenir, however, has a good balance and a sophisticated appearance. The critical difference between Avenir and Frutiger is the shape of the letter "a." The letter "a" of Avenir has good legibility. The importance of this difference becomes apparent by comparing unfamiliar names of people. This is one of the reasons why Avenir is used, not only for headlines, but also for the body text of Western magazines and newspapers.

Avenir means "the future" in French. The typeface was given its name to challenge Futura, which also means "the future" in Latin. In earlier days, Avenir's primary drawback was that there was no apparent difference between the six different weights. Adrian Frutiger and I realized the necessity of redesigning Avenir to bring out its intrinsic advantages and held many meetings to discuss our principle for reviving the typeface. In the revived version of Avenir, we created greater variation in the thickness of each weight and considerably improved the design for the italic type. In the beginning of the project, after we came up with the concept of redesigning Avenir, we decided to add small caps and condensed types. Also, Frutiger designed a new set of old-style figures, which book designers had been requesting.

I did the actual work of reviving Avenir and sent a sample to be checked by Frutiger in Switzerland. Then I redesigned according to his feedback. By repeating this process, it took us about a year and a half to complete the design of Avenir Next. I have just returned from Interlachen, Switzerland, where I directly handed a brochure of the just completed Avenir Next typeface to Frutiger. With a smile on his face, Adrian told the staff members from Linotype Library and other agents from all over the world that he liked Avenir Next the most among the typefaces he has created.

Excerpted from *Idea* no. 305, July 2004

Avenir
Next
& Avenir Next Condensed

Futura

ABCDEFG
abcdefgjpy

ao

Najib Balala
Silja Kammann
Sabine Naujoks
Jiafu Wang
Patrick Wong

Avenir Next

ABCDEFG
abcdefgjpy

ao

Najib Balala
Silja Kammann
Sabine Naujoks
Jiafu Wang
Patrick Wong

Avenir Next Ultralight
Avenir Next Regular
Avenir Next Medium
Avenir Next Demi
Avenir Next Bold
Avenir Next Heavy

Abc 1234567890

1
Alphabet specimen:
the Avenir Next family in
comparison to Futura.

2
Frutiger and Kobayashi.

3
Adrian Frutiger drawing
Avenir Next.

2

3

Matthew Carter

Interview by Joshua Berger

Yale University School of Art

Matthew Carter is one of the preeminent contemporary typographers. His work is both ubiquitous (his typefaces Georgia and Verdana were commissioned by Microsoft and now grace computer screens around the world) and revolutionary (his Walker Art Center commission resulted in the creation of a series of alphabets with "detachable" serifs). Carter has been involved in typography in one way or another for most of his life. He has lived through the passing of numerous typographic eras, and at each juncture he has embraced both the latest technology and the new forms created by young designers. In addition to teaching in the graphic design department at Yale University School of Art, Carter operates Carter & Cone, a typographic studio and consultancy based in Boston.

You have had a lifelong passion for typography. When did you know that type was your calling?

My father, Harry Carter, was a practical typographer and a historian of type. He did not push me to follow in his footsteps, but since I had read the books and met the people since childhood, I became interested in calligraphy and printing without any paternal prompting. When I left school in 1955, I had a year to fill before starting at university. Because my father had a long-standing friendship with the Enschedé printing company in the Netherlands, I was sent there as an unpaid trainee. Enschedé was very unusual in having their own type foundry on the premises (most printers ceased to make their own type as soon as typefounding became a separate trade in the sixteenth century). Enschedé's punchcutter, Paul Rädisch, had produced there the typefaces of Jan van Krimpen, the resident designer. Although the plan was to spend time in all the different departments at Enschedé, I happened to start in the type foundry, and got so interested in punchcutting and matrix-making that I spent the whole year doing that. Once I got back home to England, intending to go to university and get on with the serious business of life, I found that I had lost interest in academic study and wanted instead to make type (designing it came later). So the interlude of a year in Holland ended up determining how I've spent my life since then.

Your career has spanned nearly every phase of recent type history from hot metal to digital. Tell me about the importance of the vernacular of experience to what you do today.

Because I was born when I was, it has been possible for me to make type by essentially all the methods ever used – metal by hand, metal by machine, photoset, digital, desktop, screen – including wood, for which I got a commission recently. If you give to everything that goes into designing a typeface a score of ten, the technical aspect rates about a one or two on the same scale. In other words, at least 80-90 percent of designing type is the same regardless of whatever tool is used to make it and whatever tool is used to set it. There are, of course, a few exceptions where an inhospitable technical environment has a greater influence; Bell Centennial because of the conditions of directory production, and Verdana because of the inadequate resolution of computer monitors. But these are apart from the normal repertory of mainstream typography.

For me, the biggest change was from metal to photo, three dimensions to two, in the '60s. Photocomposition is regarded nowadays as a blip between the major forms of type, metal and digital, but in fact the change to photo felt like a more radical departure than the later change to digital. Many of the properties that are now thought of as innovative in digital type existed in photo – kerning tables, for one thing.

For a broader design audience, can you talk about how you see a knowledge of type history informing or not informing current trends in typography?

I suppose most graphic designers and typographers have a general notion that much of our pluralistic repertory of typefaces has been inherited from the past. But if you conducted a poll of the AIGA membership I think very few designers would know Garamond's first name, his dates, the significance of his work, or which current revivals have any resemblance to the original. I don't fault this; any Garamond type stands or falls by its usefulness today; its pedigree is less important. Since the early '90s when there was an explosion of experimental type design, the pendulum has swung to a more traditional emphasis. One can see this in the success of the Emigre faces Mrs. Eaves and Philosophia, which have an admitted – if eccentric – derivation from Baskerville and Bodoni. Their popularity may owe something to the idea that because they have roots they are more sober and legible than designs that have been conjured out of thin air.

I recall a conversation between yourself and Erik Spiekermann in an early '90s issue of *Eye*. One of the things that impressed me at the time was your utter openness not just to new technology, but to the resulting typographic experiments happening at the time. The dissemination of technology to a wide audience seemed to be something that excited rather than threatened you. How do you maintain this open attitude? And, ten years later, can you reflect on the state of typographic innovation? Have more designers become serious typographers?

My attitude to these things is not a considered one. If I'm less of a designosaur than people expect of somebody my age, I'm glad, but it's not a deliberate pose. As far as the technological evolution is concerned, I had to move with the times because I was employed by companies that were heavily involved in researching and developing those new technologies, and I like working with engineers. If you compare the typography of fifty years ago as I first knew it – metal type and letterpress printing – to what it has since become, there have clearly been gains and losses. For me, as somebody who thinks of himself more as a typefounder than a designer, the gains far outweigh the losses. If I had my choice of any period in the history of typography to work in, I would unhesitatingly choose the one I happen to have lucked into. Although, as I said above, I'm not a believer in "technodeterminism" and I tend to downplay the effects of technology on design, I do regard the current digital technology as the best ever and am constantly grateful for it.

You have been involved in the Yale design program for many years. What typographic notions and ideas do you believe are most critical to pass on to young designers today?

The class I teach at Yale is in type design. I teach it in tandem with Tobias Frere-Jones; he does the first semester, I do the second. It has never been the aim of the class to produce professional type designers – and so far as I know it never has. The class was started by Alvin Eisenman twenty-five years ago as part of his wish to give students a "smattering of ignorance" about the raw materials of graphic design. The aim, therefore, is to demystify type and how it's made with the idea that a more intimate knowledge will help in using it well. Chancellor Bismarck said about the law and sausages that it is better not to know how they are made, and he would probably have said the same about type. But I like to know how things are made, and I enjoy explaining the nuts and bolts of type to students. The emphasis of the class is not on production (there is no set goal in terms of number of characters completed or other benchmark), but many students achieve typefaces that are fully usable, and some continue to work on them and with them after the class ends.

Let's also discuss the typefaces featured in this book – first, Bell. How did this project come about? What was the brief for it and how long did it take to create? What were the parameters of usage?

Mergenthaler Linotype produced the typeface Bell Gothic in 1937 for setting the U.S. telephone directories. In the 1970s, AT&T began to use the pioneering high-speed digital typesetting systems to accelerate production. It was immediately obvious that Bell Gothic performed badly under these new conditions, mostly because it was too light to be legible. AT&T came back to Mergenthaler to commission a replacement for Bell Gothic that would be designed for printability. The brief also required the new typeface to be no wider than Bell Gothic, so there would be no loss of space. In the end there was a saving in space, which made Bell Centennial very popular with the directory companies for economic reasons. In the 1970s nobody thought about ecological issues such as saving trees, but they did think about saving the paper bill.

AT&T made the first approach to Mergenthaler in 1974. We made the first presentation of our design ideas in March 1976. Bell Centennial was released in 1978 (the centenary year of the U.S. directories, hence the name).

Was your creative process different or similar to other typefaces? How was it tested prior to implementation?

The early work on Bell Centennial was done for simplicity's sake on a conventional phototypesetter, Linotype's V-I-P. But since the point of the design was its suitability for digital setting I had to teach myself to work digitally. At that time there were no computer tools that could convert an analog image into a digital bitmap (the rasterization that we now take for granted as a real-time part of digital typesetting had not been invented). I had, therefore, to draw every single character on quadrille paper, pixel by pixel. Having done that, I had to encode every character by counting and entering at a keyboard the turn-on and turn-off points of every scan line – all this multiplied by the four faces that made up the Bell Centennial family: Name & Number, Address, Caption, Bold Listing. This was an epic task of hands-on designing, but it paid off in the control it allowed me over the result, not to mention in the education it gave me.

To guide the project AT&T set up a committee of directory managers, scientists from Bell Labs, quality control experts from Western Electric, and others. Normally designers will do anything to avoid working for a committee but this was the exception; the committee's involvement was crucial, particularly in making trial proofs at every stage under real production conditions.

I recall hearing Jeff Keedy talk about his typeface Keedy Sans — witnessing its appearance on McDonald's tray liners and in other ubiquitous places — all far removed from his original purpose and intent. Bell was developed before digital type became prevalent, however it is now widely distributed and used in many ways. Can you reflect on the trajectory of Bell since it was digitized? What are its limitations? Have you seen uses that surprised you? Offended you? Excited you?

I'm generally philosophical about what happens to my typefaces once they get out in the world, and I don't agonize too much over examples of misuse. Because it was designed to be printed at 6-point on high-speed presses on newsprint, the letterforms of Bell Centennial contain various devices that compensate for these extreme conditions, a form of damage control. If the letterforms are enlarged to a size where these compensatory quirks become obvious they look distorted, a sort of weirdness that certain typographers find irresistible. When the type designer Christian Schwartz enlarged Bell Centennial he thought it "looked as crazy as any mid-1990s postmodern experiment." In Christian's excellent typeface Amplitude, recently released, he has adapted the "crazy" quirks and made a virtue of what in Bell Centennial was a necessity.

You did a typeface called Wiredbaum. I read a comment from John Plunkett, the *Wired* art director at the time, that the original Walbaum was not readable enough in text. Did you agree with his assessment that the original Walbaum had legibility problems? What improvements and alterations did you make?

Late in 1994 I got a call from John Plunkett, art director of *Wired* magazine. He told me he had been using Walbaum as a text face, and in spite of changing its tracking and horizontal scaling in Quark, he and the editor had regretfully decided that it didn't work. He asked me to recommend an alternative text face. Since I, like John, am fond of Walbaum, I suggested that it might not be Walbaum's fault it was performing badly, that the problem might be one of typefounding rather than design in the sense that the off-the-shelf font he was using might not be at its best in the text of a magazine. I did a trial font based on Walbaum in which I adjusted all the variables that control a typeface's performance at a specific size: overall weight, thick-thin contrast, width, fitting, and so on. This time-honored typefounding practice, sometimes called optical scaling, got left behind when phototypesetting machines gained the ability to set all sizes from a single master, but it is worth doing when a face is only needed in a single size and can afford to be optimized for it. Faces like Walbaum that show a big contrast between thick and thin strokes benefit more from reinterpretation as size-related "cuts" than a monoline sans serif, say, that is inherently more versatile. John Plunkett liked the redrawn Walbaum; I completed what became known as Wiredbaum Roman and Italic. *Wired* used it thereafter.

walbaum	18pt.	8pt.

ABCDEFGJKLMNOPQURSTUVWXYZ
abcdefghijklmnopqurstuvwxyz
0123456789

I did a trial font based on Walbaum in which I adjusted all the variables that control a typeface's performance at a specific size: overall weight, thick-thin contrast, width, fitting, and so on. This time-honored typefounding practice, sometimes called optical scaling, got left behind when phototypesetting machines gained the ability to set all sizes from a single master, but it is worth doing when a face is only needed in a single size and can afford to be optimized for it. Faces like Walbaum that show a big contrast between thick and thin strokes benefit more from reinterpretation as size-related "cuts" than a monoline sans serif, say, that is inherently more versatile.

wiredbaum	18pt.	8pt.

ABCDEFGJKLMNOPQURSTUVWXYZ
abcdefghijklmnopqurstuvwxyz
0123456789

I did a trial font based on Walbaum in which I adjusted all the variables that control a typeface's performance at specific size: overall weight, thick-thin contrast, width, fitting, and so on. This time-honored typefounding practice, sometimes called optical scaling, got left behind when phototypesetting machines gained the ability to set all sizes from a single master, but it is worth doing when a face is only needed in a single size and can afford to be optimized for it. Faces like Walbaum that show a big contrast between thick and thin strokes benefit more from reinterpretation as size-related "cuts" than a monoline sans serif, say, that is inherently more versatile.

TQNkswg45

1

2

3

1
Wiredbaum in comparison to Walbaum.

2
Title: Wiredbaum type design
Format: Typeface
Studio: Carter & Cone
Art Director: John Plunkett
(*Wired*)
Designer: Matthew Carter
Client: *Wired* magazine
Typeface: Wiredbaum

3
Bell Centennial in use. A page from the telephone directory.

Akzidenz Grotesk

Designed by Günter Gerhard Lange

Purpose

For large signage; as an all-purpose font for print media

History

In the 1920s, Jan Tschichold described sans serif type as "a functional style for a rational era." So it is no surprise that the German typeface Akzidenz ("trade type") Grotesk (sans serif) was favored by Tschichold and his Bauhaus cohorts for its simplicity. While Akzidenz was originally featured as a display face, the lowercase would later be used for text. And though some type theorists believe that Akzidenz Grotesk was cut by anonymous punchcutters from the Berthold foundry, this useful font has also been attributed to German typographer Günter Gerhard Lange. What we can be sure of is that Akzidenz was ahead of its time, laying the foundation for other innovative fonts such as Univers and Helvetica.

Sample

Akzidenz Grotesk Roman   40 pt

abcdefghijklmnopqrstuv
wxyzABCDEFGHIJKLM
NOPQRSTUVWXYZ
1234567890

Work

1
Title: *Picture This*
Format: Exhibition catalog and poster
Studio: Pentagram
Art Director: Angus Hyland
Designers: Angus Hyland, Charlie Smith
Client: The British Council
Typeface: Akzidenz Grotesk

Pentagram wanted this catalog to "recall both the format and feel of a British tabloid newspaper" – thus, Akzidenz Grotesk.

2
Title: Times Square 2002
Format: Annual report
Studio: Worldstudio
Art Director: Mark Randall
Designer: Daniela Koenn
Photographers: Marcel Hornung,
Nelson Bakerman
Client: Times Square Alliance
Typeface: Akzidenz Grotesk

"We selected Akzidenz Grotesk for the annual report because it was clean and modern, yet still friendly. Since the report has so many statistics, we especially liked the simple playfulness of the numbers."

3
Title: De Balie
Format: Logo and monthly calendar
Studio: Thonik®
Art Director: Thonik®
Designer: Thonik®
Photographer: Thonik®
Client: De Balie Amsterdam
Typeface: Akzidenz Grotesk

Thonik® tends to use Avenir almost exclusively on their projects, but for Dutch political and cultural center De Balie's new logo, they placed the two words together in lowercase Akzidenz Grotesk instead.

1

Times Square BID
Annual Report

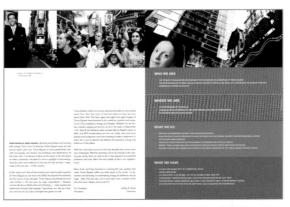

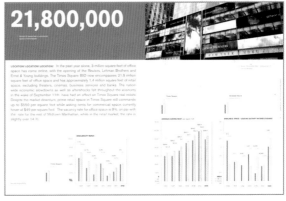

2

3

Work

4
Title: *Ray Gun*, Curve
Format: Magazine article
Art Director: Chris Ashworth
Designer: Chris Ashworth
Client: *Ray Gun* magazine
Typeface: Akzidenz Grotesk

5
Title: *Ray Gun*, Massive Attack
Format: Magazine article
Art Director: Chris Ashworth
Designer: Chris Ashworth
Client: *Ray Gun* magazine
Typeface: Akzidenz Grotesk

6
Title: Utilitarian Greeting Cards
Format: Greeting cards
Studio: Foundation 33
Art Director: Daniel Eatock
Designer: Daniel Eatock
Client: Foundation 33
Typeface: Akzidenz Grotesk

One of a set of four greeting cards
that allows the sender to customize
a message. "I use Akzidenz Grotesk
as a default font. It is a decision
that I apply to all projects, which
enables me to start working without
the dilemma of making a subjective
choice of selecting a typeface."

4

5

Greeting Card

Using a red pen delete all descriptions that are not relevant to card's recipient.

Mum	Cousin	Enemy
Dad	Nephew	Stranger
Daughter	Niece	Teacher
Son	Twin	Boss
Sister	Girlfriend	Neighbour
Brother	Boyfriend	Other*
Grandma	Wife	
Grandad	Husband	
Aunt	Friend	
Uncle	Lover	

*Please specify —

....

6

7

Title: David Byrne, *Look into the Eyeball*
Format: CD packaging
Studio: Doyle Partners
Creative Director: Stephen Doyle
Designers: Ariel Apte, John Clifford
Photographer: Stephen Doyle
Client: Virgin Records America
Typeface: Akzidenz Grotesk

8

Title: *Make It Bigger*
Format: Book
Studio: Pentagram Design
Art Director: Paula Scher
Designers: Paula Scher, Sean Carmody,
Tina Chang, Keith Daigle
Client: Princeton Architectural Press
Typeface: Akzidenz Grotesk

Scher used Akzidenz Grotesk "for its easy readability and its capacity to look both approachable and aggressive at the same time."

7

8

Work

9
Title: Fietstocht door Vinex-locaties
Den Haag (A Bike Tour through VINEX
Locations in The Hague)
Format: Map
Studio: LUST
Designer: LUST
Client: Wils&Co, Architectural Platform
of The Hague (The Hague)
Typeface: Akzidenz Grotesk

LUST used Akzidenz Grotesk Bold on
these cycling tour maps "to balance
the colorful character of the map, but at
the same time to offer sturdiness to the
surrounding white of the map."

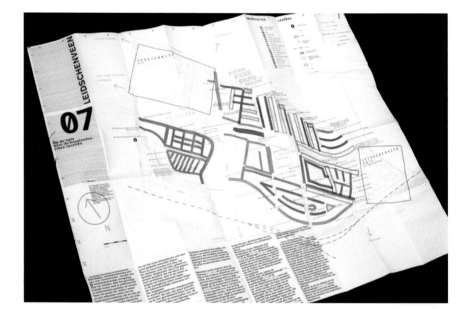

9

10

10
Title: Zumtobel
Format: Annual report
Studio: Sagmeister, Inc.
Art Director: Stefan Sagmeister
Designers: Stefan Sagmeister,
Matthias Ernstberger
Photographer: Bela Borsodi
Prototype: Joe Stone
Client: Zumtobel AG
Typeface: Akzidenz Grotesk

11
Title: Frost Design Website
Format: Website
Studio: Frost Design
Art Director: Vince Frost
Designers: Vince Frost/Frost Design,
Fred Flade/de-construct
Photographer: Alan Batham
Client: Frost Design
Typeface: Akzidenz Grotesk Super

Frost Design used only one typeface
(Akzidenz Grotesk), one color, and no
imagery in their new website design
in order to represent "Frost's strong
typographic approach to design."

11

Avenir

Designed by Adrian Frutiger

Sample

For books with a large amount of text

History

"Avenir is intended to be nothing more or less than a clear and clean representation of modern typographical trends, giving the designer a typeface which is strictly modern and at the same time human, i.e., suitably refined and elegant for use in texts of any length," said Adrian Frutiger of his design for the font. Released in 1988 by Linotype-Hell AG, Avenir was inspired by Erbar and Futura, two preexisting sans serif typefaces. While the weights of these three fonts are similar, Avenir is unique in that each of its varieties is designed for a different purpose. The result: versatile yet consistent type for a range of printing conditions.

Sample

Avenir Roman   40 pt

abcdefghijklmnopqrst
uvwxyzABCDEFGHIJK
LMNOPQRSTUVWXYZ
1234567890

Work

1
Title: *Diskó Pönk*
Format: Book
Studio: Ármann Agnarsson
Designer: Ármann Agnarsson
Typefaces: Avenir, Serifa

Avenir graces this book about the disco and punk scene in Iceland from 1977 to 1982.

2 . 3
Title: *Death Is a Process*
Format: Book
Studio: Ármann Agnarsson
Designer: Ármann Agnarsson
Typeface: Avenir Black

Here, Avenir Black is used in a "countdown" project about the human body and the process of decay.

1

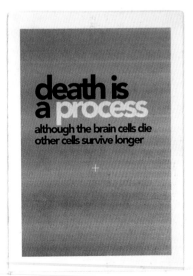

2

3

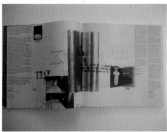

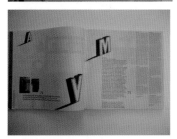

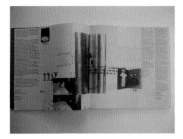

4

Title: HKA Information Catalog for
Academy of Art Arnhem
Format: Catalog
Studio: LUST
Art Director: LUST
Designer: LUST
Photographer: Ivonne Zijp
Client: HKA (Academy of Art Arnhem)
Typeface: Avenir

"Although it was set in a small size
and in light gray, Avenir, thanks to its
geometric foundation, still stays
very legible."

5

Title: Quincy
Format: Poster
Studio: Base
Art Director: Base
Designer: Base
Client: Quincy
Typeface: Avenir

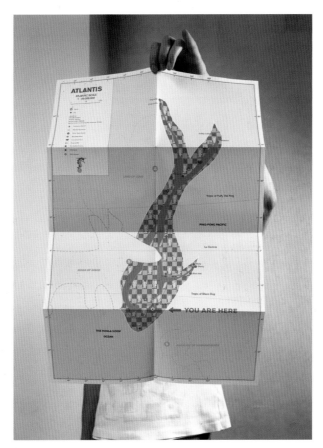

4

5

Work

6
Title: Avenir Utopia
Format: Postcard
Studio: LSD
Art Directors: Sonia Diaz,
Gabriel Martinez
Designers: Sonia Diaz,
Gabriel Martinez
Client: LSDspace
Typeface: Avenir

The designers manipulated Avenir
slightly to produce this postcard –
one in a series that utilizes fonts as
a springboard for political and social
messages.

7
Title: *Less & More*
Format: Book
Studio: Thonik®
Art Director: Thonik®
Designer: Thonik®
Client: 010 Publishers, Rotterdam
Typeface: Avenir

Dutch design studio Thonik®'s work
is "heavily conceptual: we don't want
the design to stand in the way of the
concept." Thus, they usually use only
one type: Avenir.

8
Title: *Apples & Oranges*
Format: Book
Studio: Thonik®
Art Director: Thonik®
Designer: Thonik®
Client: BIS Publishers, Amsterdam
Typeface: Avenir

O PATR▪OT▪SMO É S▪NTOMA DE ENFERM▪DADE ESTÉT▪CA, PORQUE TRANSFORMA O HÁB▪TO EM ALGO M▪STER▪OSO.(…)

Aven▪r Utop▪a / www.lsdspace.com   V▪lem Flusser, "Estrange▪ros no Mundo"

6

7

8

Title: Centraal Museum
Format: Corporate identity
Studio: Thonik®
Art Director: Thonik®
Designer: Thonik®
Client: Centraal Museum, Utrecht
Typeface: Avenir

centraal museum krant

Open, open!!

Open, open, open open o-
pen, open! Open, open open!

pagina 3, 5, 6, 7, 9

Ingmar Heytze

Van dolhuis tot doolhof

pagina 6, 7

Erich Wichman

'Ik zou een omweg maken,
om niet langs Utrecht te
hoeven'

pagina 8

C C **GRATIS**
C
C C **Nr 3** najaar 99

centraal   Nicolaaskerkhof 10
museum   3512 XC Utrecht

OPEN OPEN OPEN

Open, open open open open, open!

Open, open open! Open! Open!
open, open, open! Open open, o-
pen open! Open! open! Open o-
pen open open, open! Open! open
open! Open!!!
Open open open open. Open, open
open Open! Open! Open. Open, open, o-
pen! Open open open! Open, open!
Open! Open! open, open, open open.

Open! Open! open, open, open open.
Open! Open, open open! Open! Open!
open, open, open! Open open, open.O-
pen! Open open open open, open! Open!
open! Open!
Open! Open, open, open! Open open
open! Open open, open! Open open o-
pen open! Open, open! Open open, open!
Open! Open open open open, open! O-

pen. Open! Open! Open, open, open! O-
pen. Open. Open, open, open!

Open! Open! Open!

Open! open! open, open! Open. Open
open open open! Open, open, open! O-
pen open open! open! Open, open, O-
Open open open open! Open, open! open!
Open! Open! open, open, open open o-

pen! Open, open open. Open! Open!
open, Open open open open! Open, open
open. Open, open open open open! Open,
open, open! Open open open open! Open,
open Open!!!
Open! Open! open, open, open open. O-
pen! Open, open open! Open. Open! Open!
open, open! Open open,open!

Bell Centennial

Designed by Matthew Carter

Purpose

For listings and very poor printing conditions

History

Designed by Matthew Carter in 1978 for the AT&T Corporation, Bell Centennial marked the company's one-hundredth anniversary. A textbook example of highly skilled if inconspicuous type design, Bell Centennial evolved from the earlier Bell Gothic, designed by Mergenthaler Linotype's Chauncey H. Griffith. Bell Gothic was used in American telephone directories until the 1970s, when new printing technology compromised its legibility. Carter rendered Bell Centennial more legible and in the process, according to designer Gunnlaugur Briem, he "created a bulletproof rhinoceros that could dance *Swan Lake*."

Sample

abcdefghijklmnopqrstu
vwxyzABCDEFGHIJKLM
NOPQRSTUVWXYZ
1234567890

Work

1
Title: Bell Centennial Type Study
Format: Print
Designer: Matthew Carter
Client: Bell Telephone
Typeface: Bell Centennial

A board highlighting Matthew Carter's process
in developing the Bell Centennial typeface.

2
Title: Move Me
Format: Brochure
Studio: Alexander Isley Inc. and the Dave and
Alex Show (a joint venture)
Creative Directors: Alexander Isley, Dave
Goldenberg
Art Director: Alexander Isley
Designer: Tracie Rosenkopf-Lissauer
Photographer: John Madere
Client: Modem Media
Typefaces: Bell Centennial, Garamond

1

2

3

Title: *In Magazine*
Format: Print publication
Studio: focus2
Art Director: Todd Hart
Designer: Duane King
Photographers: Various
Client: Cantoni
Typefaces: Bell Centennial, DIN Mittelschrift

Bell Centennial was selected for its legibility
and durability in the printing process.

3

Work

4 . 5
Title: *WWD*
Art Director: Pao & Paws
Designers: Hideko Narisada, Aya Naito
Photographers: Various
Typeface: Bell Centennial

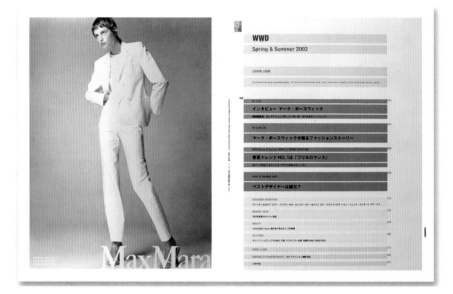

MEN'S

BEST TREND

2002 SPRING & SUMMER

2002年春夏メンズのベストトレンドはこれだ！

DENIM DISH
デニムな気分盛り

GRAPHIC JAM
グラフィックプリントの斬新な気分サリ

COAT WARFARE
スプリングコートは必須アイテム

WHITE & WHITE
静かのフッシー、ホワイト

RUFFLES AND RIDGES
ラッフル使いでセクシー

BOXING MODE
スポーツモードの歩き方 ボクシング

KAKIMOTO ARMS

カキモトアームズ

WWD-J CAFE

COLLECTION PREVIEW

季節の始まりを告げるルイ・ヴィトンのマーク・ジェイコブス

LVMH, JACOBS SIGN 7-YEAR DEAL

DO THE RITE THING

WELCOME, ALBER

04

Bell Gothic

Designed by Chauncey H. Griffith

Purpose

For very small text containing large amounts of information

History

The forerunner to Bell Centennial, Chauncey H. Griffith's Bell Gothic
was designed in 1937 for use in American telephone directories.
Prior to 1937, telephone books were printed in a variety of typefaces.
Highly legible, Bell Gothic created eminently readable blocks of text
and is still ideal for communicating large amounts of information
on a single page. The font regained popularity in the nineties, with
Architectural Record debuting a redesign that prominently featured
Bell Gothic in its logo.

Sample

Bell Gothic Bold   40 pt

abcdefghijklmnopqrstuv
wxyzABCDEFGHIJKLM
NOPQRSTUVWXYZ
1234567890

Work

1 . 2
Title: Gensfleisch,
Gastronomy-Corporate
Studio: i_d buero
Client: Morlock Enterprises
Typefaces: Bell Gothic, Clarendon

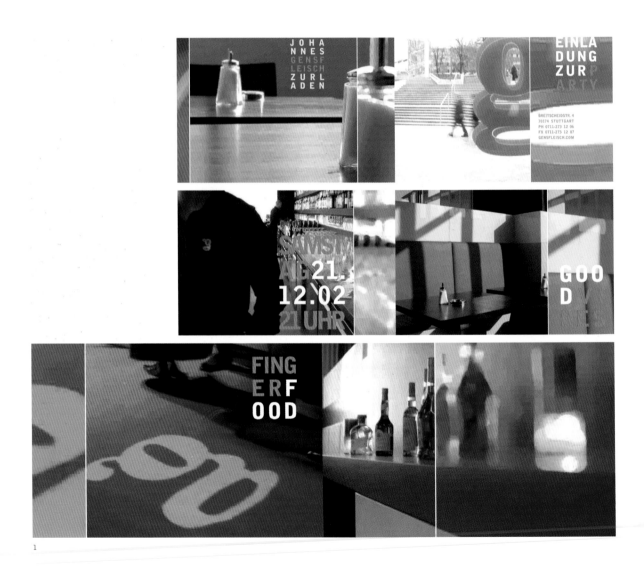

1

2

Work

5 . 6 . 7
Title: Milk Studios
Format: Corporate identity
Studio: Base
Designer: Base
Photographers: Various
Client: Milk Studios
Typeface: Bell Gothic

Base customized Bell Gothic for this
photography studio "because of its direct
link to the logo, as well as its ability to
'soften' the other elements around it."

8
Title: 21st Century Cities Convention
Format: Poster
Studio: Bis]
Art Director: Bis]
Designers: Àlex Gifreu, Pere Alvaro
Client: Catalonia's Architect Organization
Typeface: Bell Gothic

"The linear grid used to represent the urban
plan of the city was well complemented by
the straight lines of Bell Gothic."

5

450 West 15th Street
New York, NY 10011
Telephone 212 645 2797
Fax 212 645 2843
Email milk.compuserve.com

Milk Studios

6

New York's premier superstudio
45,000 sq. ft. divided over five studios
Natural daylight
In-house equipment
Location services
Digital services
Onsite café, bar and catering

450 West 15th Street New York, NY 10011 Telephone 212 645 2797 www.milkstudios.com

Milk Studios

7

CICLE DE CONFERÈNCIES

CIUTATS DEL SEGLE XXI   D'ABRIL A DESEMBRE DE 2002   COL·LEGI D'ARQUITECTES DE CATALUNYA

RIO DE JANEIRO > MEXICO > BERLIN > NEW YORK > ROMA > TOKIO > MADRID

DIRECCIÓ: *JORDI BORJA*, COORDINACIÓ: *ZAIDA MUXÍ*

8

DIN

Designed by Wagner

Purpose

For signage, posters, and displays

History

DIN, or Deutsche Industrie-Norm, is the collection of typefaces used on the majority of road signs and license plates in the former West Germany. But DIN's history actually lies in the earliest monotone letterforms (those featuring strokes of even thickness) from Ancient Greece (fifth to second century B.C.). It is from these forms that we get the term "Grotesque," i.e., sans serif. Designed by Wagner in 1932, the DIN family was inspired by Akzidenz Grotesk letterforms. Four geometric sans serif typefaces comprise the family and are valued for their simplicity and readability. Fontshop has dubbed it "the German 'Autobahn' typeface," and with the vision of Dutch designer Albert-Jan Pool, Fontshop redrew the utilitarian font for expanded use in 1995.

Sample

DIN Mittelschrift 40 pt

abcdefghijklmnopqrstuv
wxyzABCDEFGHIJKLMN
OPQRSTUVWXYZ
1234567890

Work

1
Title: Villa Celimontana Jazz
Programme
Format: Print publication
Studio: Vespina
Art Director: Nino Brisindi
Designer: Nino Brisindi
Client: Villa Celimontana Jazz Festival
Typeface: DIN Engschrift

DIN Engschrift was used for its
"simplicity, modern sight, readability
(also in a vertical orientation)."

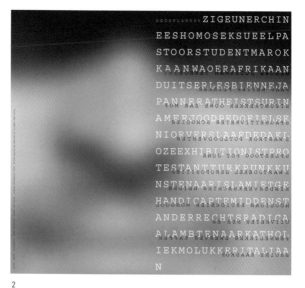

2

1

3

Räät mee over a uue het oopa nieuwe l Europa

Waar ligt Estland?

12.september / De Maatschappij voor Oude en Nieuwe Media, Nieuwmarkt 4, Amsterdam
15.15 – 16.15u / Discussie met:
Eousewies van der Laan (Europarlementariër, D66)
László Marácz (Oost-Europa deskundige), härra Dick Benschop'iga
Henk Raaff (journalist) d osaleda interneti chat'il, aadressil: **www.europa-interactief.nl**
& jonge politici
16.15 – 17.00u / Live internet-chat: **www.europa-interactief.nl**
Kom en doe mee!
Voertaal: Engels

2
Title: Tolerant Nederland
Format: Print advertising
Studio: UNA (Amsterdam) Designers
Art Director: Hans Bockting
Designer: Sabine Reinhardt
Photographer: André Thijssen
Client: FontShop BeNeLux
Typefaces: DIN Black, DIN Medium

"We were looking for a neutral font in the FontShop library and found that in DIN."

3
Title: *Blah Blah Blah* no. 1
Format: Magazine cover
Art Directors: Chris Ashworth, Neil Fletcher
Designers: Chris Ashworth, Neil Fletcher
Client: *Blah Blah Blah* magazine
Typeface: DIN Engschrift

4
Title: Europe Interactive
Format: Poster
Studio: LUST
Designer: LUST
Client: Dutch Ministry of Foreign Affairs
Typeface: DIN Mittelschrift

LUST chose DIN for this bilingual project because of the font's reputation as a "multinational standard that theoretically wouldn't 'bias' one poster over the other."

4

Work

5
Title: Mouse on Mars, *Radical Connector*
Format: CD packaging
Studio: Icon, Communications Design
Art Director: Frieda Luczak
Designer: Frieda Luczak
Client: Mouse on Mars
Typeface: FF DIN

FF DIN was used here because it is
"strong, simple, not precious."

6
Title: Sun America Affordable
Housing Partners
Format: Marketing brochure
Studio: Chase Design Group
Art Director: Margo Chase
Designer: Margo Chase
Photographer: Nick Rueschel
Client: Sun America Affordable
Housing Partners
Typeface: DIN Mittelschrift

7
Title: Sun America Affordable
Housing Partners
Format: Print advertisement
Studio: Chase Design Group
Art Director: Margo Chase
Designer: Margo Chase
Photographer: Nick Rueschel
Client: Sun America Affordable
Housing Partners
Typeface: DIN Mittelschrift

"DIN has an honest, straightforward, no-
nonsense directness that was appropriate
for the tone of this piece."

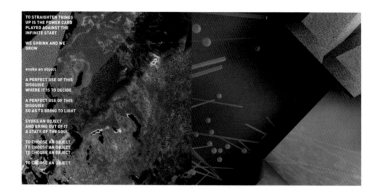

5

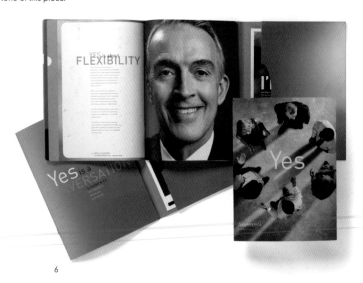

6

7

Title: Nigel Coates, *Guide to Ecstacity*
Format: Book
Studio: Why Not Associates
Designer: Why Not Associates
Photographer: Tim Kiusakaas
Client: Laurence King Publishing
Typeface: DIN Mittelschrift

"DIN Mittelschrift was used as a text font for its clean, modern feel."

Franklin Gothic

Designed by Vic Caruso

Purpose

For newspapers and where available space is limited

History

Arguably the most widely used font ever produced, Franklin Gothic was designed by Morris Fuller Benton between 1903 and 1912 for American Type Founders Company. Because of its steady popularity, the typeface was updated in 1979 for ITC by Vic Caruso. This new version included more weights and became the standard choice for newspapers and advertising. The original font takes its name from Benjamin Franklin.

Sample

Franklin Gothic Book   40 pt

abcdefghijklmnopqrstu
vwxyzABCDEFGHIJKLM
NOPQRSTUVWXYZ
1234567890

Work

1 . 2 . 3
Title: *Bill Viola*
Format: Exhibition catalog
Studio: RMCD
Art Director: Rebeca Méndez
Designer: Rebeca Méndez
Assistant Designers: Bele Duke, Susana
Van Gastel
Client: Whitney Museum of
American Art
Typeface: Franklin Gothic

Describing the typeface as having
"a clear geometry and an upfront, bold
personality," Méndez confesses: "A love
affair with Franklin Gothic was at play."

4
Title: Jobs
Format: Newspaper Op Ed
Studio: Doyle Partners
Creative Director: Stephen Doyle
Photographer: Stephen Doyle
Client: The *New York Times*
Typeface: Franklin Gothic

5
Title: "OK" Soda
Format: 12-can packaging
Studio: Wieden+Kennedy
Art Director: Todd Waterbury
Designer: Todd Waterbury
Illustrator: Daniel Clowes
Client: The Coca-Cola Company
Typefaces: Trade Gothic,
Franklin Gothic

"Trade Gothic and Franklin Gothic
were antidotes to the overdesigned,
deconstructed, drop–shadowed,
'extreme' typefaces that most youth
marketers employed at the time."

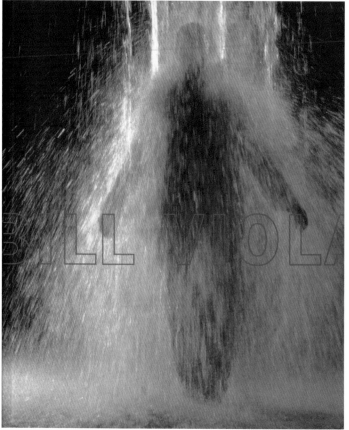

1

2

60   Interval
                    1995
         Video/sound installation

Two large color projections stand opposite each other, filling the side walls of a small room. Viewers pass between the images on their way through the space. An image of a man alone in a shower room, naked, is seen on one wall as he slowly and methodically cleans his body with a white cloth and a bucket of water. A series of wild and violent images appears on the other wall, showing a figure struggling through fire and water intercut with scenes of the camera point of view aggressively pushing itself through folds of skin into the body's orifices.

The two sets of images represent not only opposing architectural surfaces, but embody opposing energies—peaceful/violent, passive/aggressive, calm/chaotic. Controlled by a computer-programmed switcher, the images are never present on opposite walls simultaneously. Instead they appear sequentially, one at a time, displayed according to a mathematically programmed curve that alternates their duration in ever decreasing intervals of time. Starting at one minute, the images and sound switch slowly at first, then faster and faster, finally reaching the limit of the frame rate of the video signal at thirty times per second. This extreme peak condition is maintained for a few moments until both images abruptly end in black and silence and the cycle starts anew.

What begins as a simple, slow succession of images gradually becomes a violent, roaring alternation, eventually reaching a blurred merger of the two as the peak switching frequency is reached, exceeding the ability of the human eye and ear to distinguish between distinct pictures and sounds, and creating the impression that the two images are, for a brief moment, coexisting simultaneously.

3

4

5

Work

6
Title: Big Phat Democracy Party
Format: Print advertisement
Studio: Art Chantry Design Co.
Designer: Art Chantry
Client: The Committee for Big
Phat Parties
Typeface: Franklin Gothic

7
Title: *Ray Gun* pitch work
Format: Print
Art Directors: Chris Ashworth,
Neil Fletcher
Designers: Chris Ashworth,
Neil Fletcher
Client: *Ray Gun* magazine
Typefaces: Franklin Gothic, Helvetica

8
Title: MoMA Design Store Soho
Format: Brand identity
Studio: Base
Art Director: Base
Designer: Base
Photographer: Guido Mocafico
Client: Museum of Modern Art,
New York
Typeface: Franklin Gothic Heavy

"We view Franklin Gothic Heavy as
a modern interpretation of MoMA's
original Franklin Gothic logo."

6

7

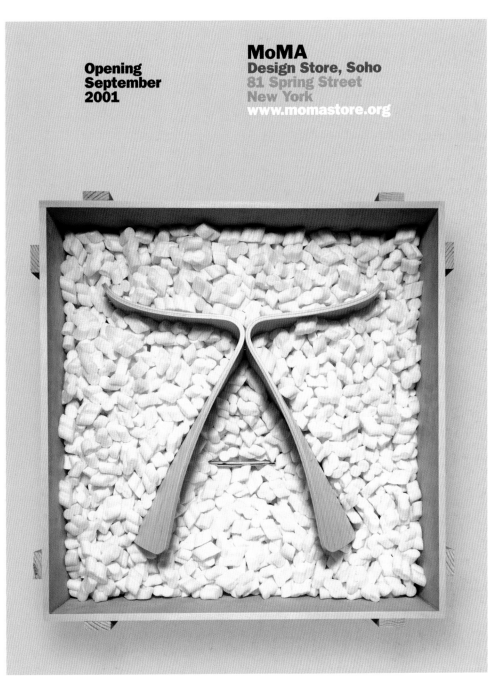

**Opening
September
2001**

MoMA
Design Store, Soho
81 Spring Street
New York
www.momastore.org

8

Work

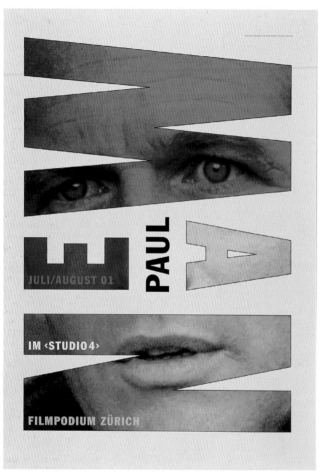

9

11

12

10

SELVÄ SUOMI 75
JULISTE
KILPAILU
25.8.–15.9.92

SUOMEN RAITTIUSJÄRJESTÖT · NUORISOKASVATUSLIITTO

9
Title: Paul Newman
Format: Silkscreened poster
Designer: Ralph Schraivogel
Client: Filmpodium Zürich
Typeface: Franklin Gothic

10
Titles: COCA Piercing Visions,
Survival Research Laboratories,
Freak House, Alternative
Bumbershoot, Gala Opening
Format: Posters
Studio: Art Chantry Design Co.
Designer: Art Chantry
Client: Center on Contemporary
Art, Seattle, WA
Typefaces: Franklin Gothic, Futura

11
Title: Boycott McGardenburger
Format: Magazine cover
Studio: Art Chantry Design Co.
Designer: Art Chantry
Client: Zach Lyons,
Boycott Quarterly
Typeface: Franklin Gothic

12
Title: Boycott Nike
Format: Magazine cover
Studio: Art Chantry Design Co.
Designer: Art Chantry
Client: Zach Lyons,
Boycott Quarterly
Typeface: Franklin Gothic

13
Title: Anti-Alcohol campaign
Format: Poster
Studio: Kari Piippo Oy
Art Director: Kari Piippo
Designer: Kari Piippo
Client: Suomen Raittiusjärjestöt
Typeface: Franklin Gothic

"The curved text in the poster
required a strong typeface
in order to be effective. Franklin
Gothic fulfilled this demand
with excellence."

13

Frutiger

Designed by Adrian Frutiger

Purpose

For large signage; as an all-purpose font for print media

History

An efficient but cheerful face, Frutiger embodies a unique
timelessness. Its origins stem from the redesign of France's
Charles de Gaulle Airport. The airport owners wanted
a new signage system that would complement the airport's
architectural overhaul. Swiss designer Adrian Frutiger of
the French foundry Deberny & Peignot designed such
a complementary font, the eponymous Frutiger, in 1976.
Frutiger's clean, robust sans serif design still offers a relaxed
appearance ideal for the juxtaposition of words and images.

Sample

Frutiger 55 Roman   40 pt

abcdefghijklmnopqrs
tuvwxyzABCDEFGHIJK
LMNOPQRSTUVWXYZ
1234567890

Work

1
Title: Frutiger's Tray
Format: Tray
Studio: Did Graphics Inc.
Art Director: Majid Abbasi
Designer: Majid Abbasi
Client: Yazdgol Household Company
Typeface: Frutiger

"The power and simplicity of this typeface is incredible."

2
Title: Abigail Kirsch
Format: Print advertising
Art Director: Anri Seki
Designer: Anri Seki
Photographer: Stock Image
Client: Abigail Kirsch
Typefaces: Frutiger, Garamond

In this case, Frutiger was the client's identity typeface "to reflect modernity and cleanness."

1

2

3

4

4
Title: *Leading Artists of POP ART*
Format: Poster
Studio: Did Graphics Inc.
Art Director: Majid Abbasi
Designer: Majid Abbasi
Client: Tehran Museum of
Contemporary Art
Typefaces: Frutiger, Helvetica

Abbasi chose Frutiger for its
"lightness" in representing the title of
the show

3 . 5 . 6
Title: *Flux* Magazine
Format: Flyers and magazines
Studio: RMCD
Art Director: Willem Henri Lucas
Designer: Willem Henri Lucas
Illustrator: Willem Henri Lucas
Client: Adam Eeuwens, Amsterdam
Typeface: Frutiger

"The magazine was all about content,
not form. The Frutiger typeface has
no character, it is the plain Jane of
lettertypes. It does not distract, does
not interfere, does not color, just
dutifully conveys."

5

6

Work

7 . 8 . 9
Title: Dentsu 2002
Format: Annual report
Studio: Dentsu, Inc.
Art Director: Takahiro Kurashima
Designers: Takahiro Kurashima,
Hiroko Tanaka
Client: Dentsu, Inc.
Typeface: Frutiger

10
Title: *Graphic Design Iran 1*
Format: Book cover
Studio: Did Graphics Inc.
Art Director: Majid Abbasi
Designer: Majid Abbasi
Photographer: Farhoud Haghi
Client: Iranian Graphic Designers
Society (IGDS)
Typeface: Frutiger

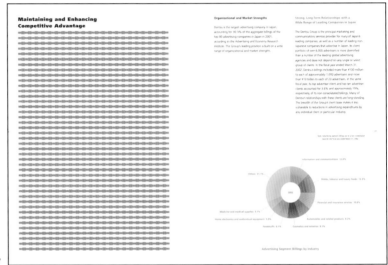

7

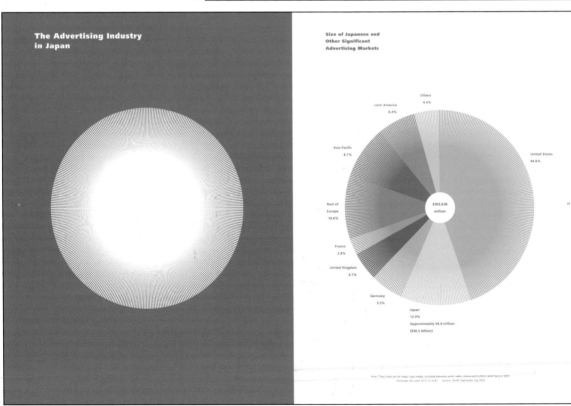

8

11
Title: Brief Encounters
Format: Poster
Studio: Did Graphics Inc.
Art Director: Majid Abbasi
Designer: Majid Abbasi
Illustrator: Majid Abbasi
Client: Thierry Sarfis
Typefaces: Helvetica, Frutiger

Abbasi worked with Frutiger because of its "simplicity" and ability to make straight lines.

12
Title: The Keystone
Format: Poster
Studio: Did Graphics Inc.
Art Director: Majid Abbasi
Designer: Majid Abbasi
Client: The 5th Color
Typefaces: Frutiger, Thulth
(Persian font)

One of the first posters Abbasi designed with Frutiger, this one relies on the font's "delicateness and simplicity."

9

10

11

12

Futura

Designed by Paul Renner

Purpose

For large displays; small text in books

History

Form follows function — it is this Bauhaus design principle that inspired the elegantly geometric sans serif type Futura. The most influential font design of the Bauhaus era, Futura is beautifully utilitarian. Designed in 1927 by Paul Renner, it is a simple geometric font. Its trademark: long ascenders and descenders. The font barely conforms to the historical shape of the letters; rather, it displays an innate radicalism that stands the test of time.

Sample

Futura Book   40 pt

abcdefghijklmnopqrstu
vwxyzABCDEFGHIJKL
MNOPQRSTUVWXYZ
1234567890

Work

1
Title: Sten A. Olssons Kulturstipendium
Format: Invitation
Studio: Io
Designer: Io
Client: Sten A. Olssons Stiftelse
Typeface: Futura Medium

2
Title: *Här Kommer de Varma Strömmarna*
Format: Book
Studio: Io
Designer: Io
Client: Alfabeta Anamma
Typeface: Futura Medium

1

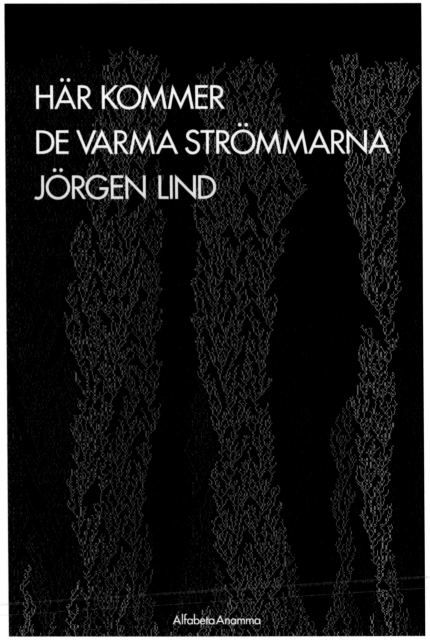

HÄR KOMMER
DE VARMA STRÖMMARNA
JÖRGEN LIND

Alfabeta Anamma

2

3

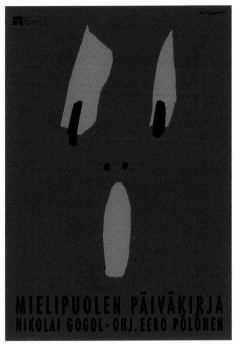

4

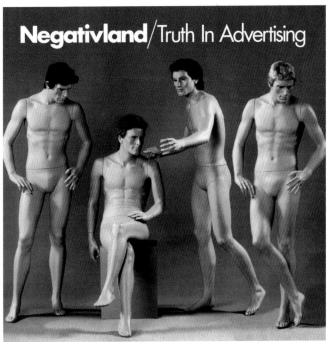

5

Work

6
Title: Jim White, *No Such Place*
Format: CD packaging
Studio: Doyle Partners
Art Directors: Paul Sahre, Jim White
Designers: Paul Sahre, Cara Brower
Photographer: André Thijssen
Client: Luaka Bop
Typeface: Futura

"It seems like Futura all caps with some letter spacing was mandatory for these types of publications," says Sahre, referring to the 1950s government documents he wanted to reference in this design.

7
Title: *Notable American Women*
Format: Book
Studio: O.O.P.S.
Creative Director: John Gall
Designer: Paul Sahre
Client: Vintage
Typeface: Futura

8
Title: Variations on a Theme by Behrizan
Format: Print advertisment
Studio: Did Graphics Inc.
Art Director: Majid Abbasi
Designer: Majid Abbasi
Photographer: Farhoud Haghi
Client: Royal Behrizan Door Handles
Typeface: Futura

"The simplicity and logical design of Futura was especially suitable for this particular advertising campaign."

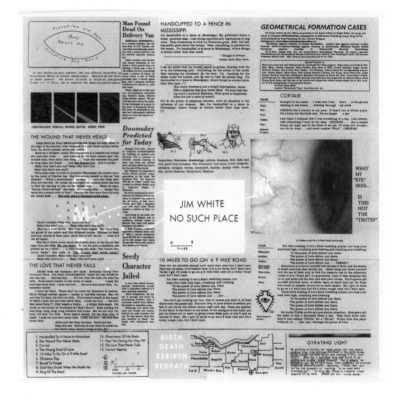

6

9
Title: *Sensation*
Format: Exhibit poster
Studio: Why Not Associates
Art Director: Why Not Associates
Designer: Why Not Associates
Photographers: Rocco Redondo,
Photodisc
Client: Royal Academy of Arts
Typeface: Futura

"Futura was used as the capital
letter 'A' worked well with
the shape of the iron, and it was
important that the word
was of roughly equal length
either side of the 'A.'"

7

8

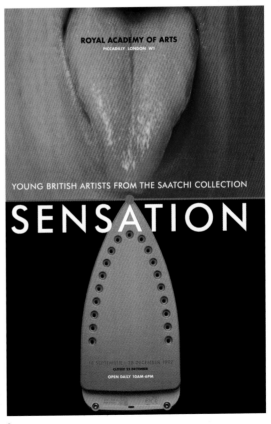

9

Gill Sans

Designed by Eric Gill

Purpose

For signage; as an all-purpose font for print media

History

Gill Sans represents traditional modernism at its best. Designed by Eric Gill and first released between 1927 and 1930, this sans serif is a stronger version of an earlier typeface designed for the London Underground by Gill's friend and teacher Edward Johnston. Gill Sans features classical proportions that are highly legible in text and display work. With its heritage in pen-written letters, Gill Sans marks a return to old forms as the basis for a twentieth-century alphabet and is classified as a humanist sans serif.

Sample

Gill Sans Regular   40 pt

abcdefghijklmnopqrstuv
wxyzABCDEFGHIJKLM
NOPQRSTUVWXYZ
1234567890

Work

1 . 2
Title: Overmis Font
Format: Typeface development
Studio: Ármann Agnarsson
Art Director: Gerad Unger
Designer: Ármann Agnarsson
Typefaces: Gill Sans, Avenir, Courier

Agnarsson calls this an "accessory
font" – designed with existing letter
forms in combination with
abstract elements.

3 . 4
Title: Lingo Dance Theater
Format: Press kit folder and
translucent insert
Studio: Piper Design Co.
Art Director: Christina Stein
Designers: Christina Stein, Brian Piper
Photographer: Matthew Cazier
Client: Lingo Dance Theater
Typeface: Gill Sans

For this contemporary dance group, the
designers chose Gill Sans "for its modernity
and varying weights."

5
Title: Art Center College of Design
Recruitment Catalog 1993–94
Format: Print publication
Studio: ACCD Design Office
Creative Director: Stuart Frolick
Design Director: Rebeca Méndez
Designer: Rebeca Méndez
Photographer: Steven A. Heller
Client: ACCD
Typeface: Gill Sans

"I chose Gill Sans as the font family for
ACCD's brand identity in 1991. The font is
beautifully geometric and sensual."

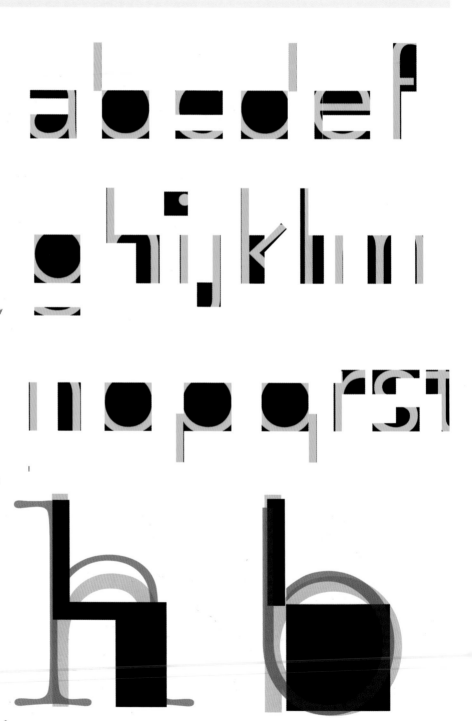

1

2

Lingo
DANCETHEATER

3

... dancetheater is a group
of inspiring contemporary
artists, athletes, actors,
bravehearts, lunatics... and,
yes dancers.

Lingo

4

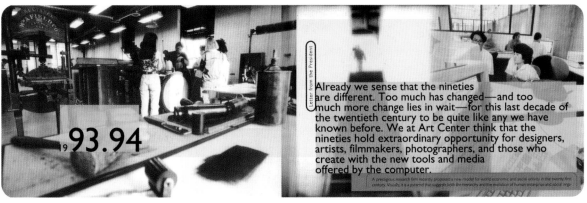

Letter from the President

19 93.94

Already we sense that the nineties
are different. Too much has changed—and too
much more change lies in wait—for this last decade of
the twentieth century to be quite like any we have
known before. We at Art Center think that the
nineties hold extraordinary opportunity for designers,
artists, filmmakers, photographers, and those who
create with the new tools and media
offered by the computer.

A prestigious research firm recently proposed a new model for world economic and social activity in the twenty-first
century. Visually, it is a pyramid that suggests both the hierarchy and the evolution of human enterprise and social organ...

5

Work

6
Title: *Death of a Salesman*
Format: Poster
Studio: Kari Piippo Oy
Art Director: Kari Piippo
Designer: Kari Piippo
Client: Mikkelin Teatteri
Typeface: Gill Sans

7
Title: *Jubilee*
Format: DVD booklet and cover
Studio: Art Chantry Design Co.
Designers: Art Chantry, Jamie Sheehan
Photographer: Matthew Cazier
Client: Susan Arosteguy, The Criterion
Collection
Typeface: Gill Sans

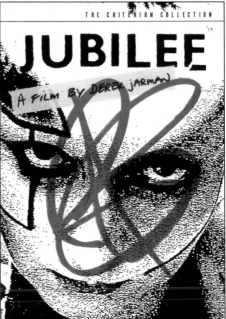

6

7

Portman
BAR MENU

8

8
Title: The Portman menu
Format: Print collateral
Studio: Social
Art Director: Paul Driver
Designer: Paul Driver
Client: Radisson SAS Hotel,
Portman London
Typeface: Gill Sans

9
Title: *Metrópoli*
Format: Magazine cover
Art Director: Rodrigo Sánchez
Designer: Rodrigo Sánchez
Client: Unidad Editorial S.A.
Typeface: Gill Sans

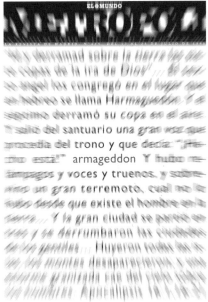

9

Helvetica

Designed by Max Miedinger

Purpose

For large or small text; as an all-purpose typeface

History

A traditional font in the nineteenth-century style, Helvetica was designed by Max Miedinger in 1957 for the Haas foundry in Basel, Switzerland. Miedinger took the Berthold Akzidenz/Standard family of the beginning of the century, which was extremely popular among Swiss typographers, and polished it up. Helvetica is now one of the most widely used type families, especially for computer applications and operating systems. Its clear and concise letterforms are flexible at any size and make it ideal for a variety of communication forms.

Sample

Helvetica Regular 40 pt

abcdefghijklmnopqrst
uvwxyzABCDEFGHIJK
LMNOPQRSTUVWXYZ
1234567890

Work

1
Title: Jazzfestival Saalfelden
Format: Print logo and publication
Studio: Automat
Art Directors: Jürgen Bauer,
Llewellen Heili
Designers: Jürgen Bauer,
Llewellen Heili
Client: Jazzfestival Saalfelden
Typeface: Helvetica

"Helvetica is a classic font capable
of modern interpretation" — just
like jazz.

2 . 3
Title: Graphic 03, File Formats/
Compression
Format: Printed promotion
Studio: Build
Art Director: Michael C. Place
Designer: Michael C. Place
Client: Magma, UK
Typeface: Helvetica 75 Bold

1

2

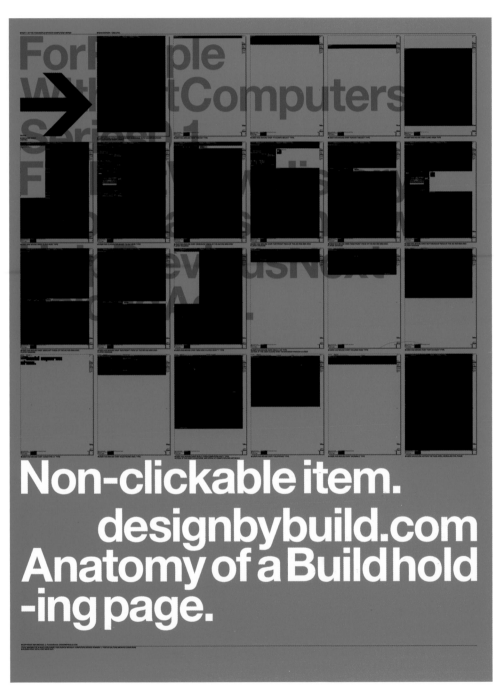

Non-clickable item.
designbybuild.com
Anatomy of a Build hold
-ing page.

Work

4
Title: The Lounge
Studio: Social
Art Director: Paul Driver
Designer: Paul Driver
Client: Radisson SAS Hotel, Leeds
Typeface: Helvetica

"Helvetica used in upper and lower
case creates a lovely balance."

5
Title: Chronological Order/Peace
and Love
Format: Poster
Studio: Build
Art Director: Michael C. Place
Designer: Michael C. Place
Client: We Love Cooking, FR
Typeface: Helvetica 75 Bold

6
Title: Safe-T UniForm
Format: Press release
Studio: Form
Art Directors: Paula Benson, Paul West
Designers: Claire Warner, Paul West
Illustrator: Claire Warner
Client: UniForm
Typeface: Helvetica Neue

7
Title: *Brooklyn Keeps On Takin' It*
Format: CD packaging
Studio: Build
Art Director: Michael C. Place
Designer: Michael C. Place
Client: Record Camp Records, USA
Typeface: Helvetica 75 Bold

4

6

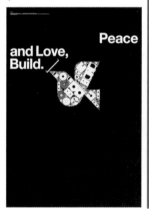

5

7

8

9

10

Work

11
Title: Royal New Zealand Ballet
Format: Tour Program
Studio: Social
Art Directors: Paul Driver,
Steven Lucker
Designer: Paul Driver
Photographers: Ross Brown,
Bill Cooper
Client: Royal New Zealand Ballet
Typeface: Helvetica

"Helvetica holds it all together.
It helped to make the program look
up-to-date, reflecting the modern
nature of the performance."

12
Title: John Ford
Format: Poster
Designer: Ralph Schraivogel
Client: Filmpodium Zürich
Typeface: Helvetica

13
Title: Plakate Schraivogel
Format: Poster
Designer: Ralph Schraivogel
Client: School of Design Bern
Typeface: Helvetica

11

12

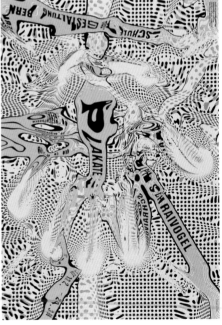

13

14

15

14
Title: *i-jusi* #13 (Bitterjusi issue)
Format: Magazine page
Studio: Orange Juice Design
Art Director: Garth Walker
Designer: Brandt Botes
Illustrator: Brandt Botes
Client: Orange Juice Design
Typefaces: Helvetica, Trade Gothic

Helvetica is used here because "the text needed to be 'non-typography.'"

15
Title: *Metrópoli*
Format: Magazine cover
Art Director: Rodrigo Sánchez
Designer: Rodrigo Sánchez
Illustrator: Rodrigo Sánchez
Client: Unidad Editorial S.A.
Typeface: Helvetica Neue Roman

16
Title: Bad Cash Quartet, *Midnight Prayer*
Format: CD packaging
Studio: Io
Art Director: Io
Designer: Io
Client: Warner Music Scandinavia
Typeface: Helvetica Neue 75 Bold

17
Title: *The Clash: Photographs by Bob Gruen*
Format: Book
Studio: Form
Art Director: Paul West
Designer: Paul West
Photographer: Bob Gruen
Client: Vision On Publishing
Typeface: Neue Helvetica Bold

18
Title: RCA Architecture Catalog
Format: Print publication
Art Directors: Eric and Marie
Designers: Eric and Marie
Client: Royal College of Art
Typeface: Helvetica

16

17

18

Meta

Designed by Eric Spiekermann

Purpose

For text and numbers, especially corporate communication

History

Originally designed by Erik Spiekermann in 1991 as a corporate font, FF Meta is appreciated by designers for its rugged charm. Hailed as "the typeface for the nineties," Meta was the logo face for *ID* magazine, a leading communication design publication of the decade. The typeface is based on an earlier font commissioned by the German Post Office (Bundepost). Meta gets its name from MetaDesign, the Berlin studio where it was developed.

Sample

MetaPlusNormal Roman 40 pt

abcdefghijklmnopqrstu
vwxyzABCDEFGHIJKLMN
OPQRSTUVWXYZ
1234567890

Work

1 . 2 . 3 . 4
Title: Simpson Center for the Humanities
Format: Posters and print collateral
Art Director: Karen Cheng
Designer: Karen Cheng
Studio: Cheng Design
Client: Simpson Center for the Humanities,
University of Washington (Seattle)
Typeface: Meta

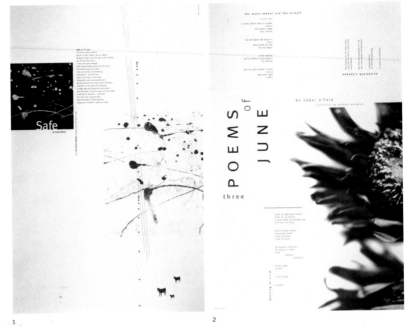

1

2

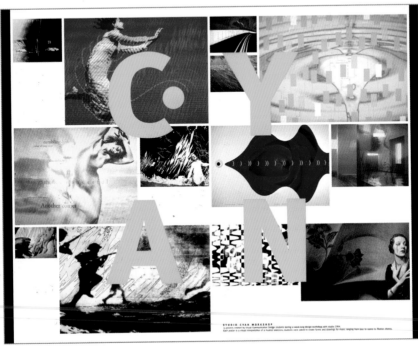

3

4

Title: *Metrópoli*
Format: Magazine cover
Art Director: Rodrigo Sánchez
Designer: Rodrigo Sánchez
Client: Unidad Editorial S.A.
Typeface: Meta

Metrópoli.

El ● Mundo. La revista de Madrid. Nº390. Del

El Amparo, Jockey, El Bodegón, Pedro

teca, El Cenador del Prado,

ueva Abuelita, Roba

Teatriz, El Chaflán, P

Nicolás,

Larumbe, Cabo Mayor, Lha

14 al 20 de Noviembre de 1997.

Abrimos las puertas de los comedores más

privados de Madrid: Zalacaín,

ador Frontón, La Gastro

Errota Zar, La N

rdy, Café de Oriente, Belagua, As

aradís Casa de América,

Gala

Para saber dónde se cuecen las decisiones más importantes.

5

Work

6 . 7
Title: Simpson Center for the Humanities
Format: Posters and print collateral
Art Director: Karen Cheng
Designer: Karen Cheng
Studio: Cheng Design
Client: Simpson Center for the Humanities,
University of Washington (Seattle)
Typeface: Meta

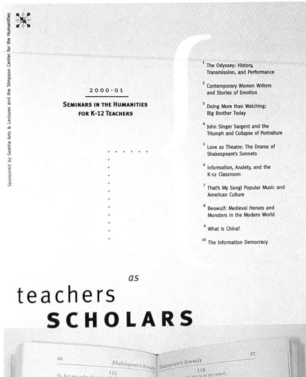

2000-01

SEMINARS IN THE HUMANITIES
FOR K-12 TEACHERS

1 The Odyssey: History,
  Transmission, and Performance

2 Contemporary Women Writers
  and Stories of Emotion

3 Doing More than Watching:
  Big Brother Today

4 John Singer Sargent and the
  Triumph and Collapse of Portraiture

5 Love as Theatre: The Drama of
  Shakespeare's Sonnets

6 Information, Anxiety, and the
  K-12 Classroom

7 That's My Song! Popular Music and
  American Culture

8 Beowulf: Medieval Heroes and
  Monsters in the Modern World

9 What is China?

10 The Information Democracy

as

teachers
SCHOLARS

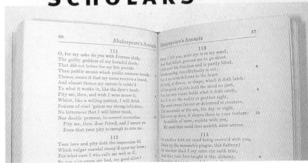

DEDICATING THE HUMANITIES

the **fall 2000** gala
NEW SIMPSON CENTER OFFICES

"What is needed by most of us is a kindling of the **desire to help the less fortunate** — the feeling that our good fortune carries with it an obligation to put something back into the community."

interview WITH A SCHOLAR

SHANNON DUDLEY
ETHNOMUSICOLOGY

DUDLEY ANALYZES STEELBAND PERFORMANCE BOTH AS A CREATIVE ART AND AS A POLITICIZED FORM OF EXPRESSION THAT REACTS TO AND DEFINES IDEAS ABOUT "CULTURE" IN TRINIDAD

CAMP STUDIES HOW ENSLAVED WOMEN FORGED CULTURES OF RESISTANCE OUT OF THEIR GENDERED EXPERIENCE OF BONDAGE

STEPHANIE CAMP
HISTORY

BRUCE BURGETT
AMERICAN STUDIES

BURGETT BELIEVES THAT TEACHING STUDENTS IS TEACHING THEM ABOUT HOW KNOWLEDGE IS CREATED AS MUCH AS IT IS ABOUT KNOWLEDGE ITSELF"

WILLIAM J. TALBOTT
PHILOSOPHY

TALBOTT EXPLAINS HUMAN RIGHTS THEORY AS THE ATTEMPT TO WORK OUT "WHAT IS THE CORRECT WAY OF GIVING APPROPRIATE CONSIDERATION TO EACH INDIVIDUAL?"

7

NEW faces

introducing KATHLEEN WOODWARD
new Simpson Center director

by Margit Dementi, Associate Director

12

Myriad

Designed by Adobe Type Staff, Carol Twombly, Christopher Slye, Fred Brady, Robert Slimbach

Purpose

For large displays; as an all-purpose font for print media

History

The result of a two-year collaboration between type designers Carol Twombly and Robert Slimbach, Myriad is a lively sans serif. Reminiscent of Frutiger, it was an especially popular typeface in the early nineties after its release in 1992 by Adobe Originals. Myriad replaced Apple Garamond as Apple's corporate font in early 2000. It is now used by Apple as its primary font for marketing materials.

Sample

Myriad Roman   40 pt

abcdefghijklmnopqrstu
vwxyzABCDEFGHIJKLMN
OPQRSTUVWXYZ
1234567890

Work

1 . 2

Title: Urban Redevelopment
Authority 2003-2004
Format: Annual report
Art Directors: Daniel Koh & Mark Lai
Designer: Daniel Koh
Illustrator: Daniel Koh
Photographer: Wai Teik Photography
Client: Urban Redevelopment
Authority Singapore
Typefaces: Myriad, Eidetic Neo

Myriad was chosen for "its
contemporary and timeless
appearance. It has a humanist
touch to it, too."

URA SPIRIT

Our values are reflected in the URA SPIRIT.
We have a strong culture of achieving work
excellence through the URA SPIRIT.
Together, the URA SPIRIT guides
our daily interactions in the office and
with our customers.

"URA" defines how we work.

UNLEARN We consciously re-examine what we do, and how and why we do it. We learn from our mistakes and failures, and where necessary, we unlearn what we have learnt.

REINVENT We are not afraid to remake URA in order to stay ahead.

ACHIEVE We work hard to achieve our mission of making Singapore a great city in which to live, work and play.

"SPIRIT" stands for our core values.

SERVICE We serve the community with commitment, sincerity and empathy. We anticipate and respond to their needs. We constantly look for new and better ways to deliver our products and services.

PASSION We perform our duties with passion because we are creating a legacy for future generations. We persevere in the face of setbacks and take pride in our work. We do not settle for anything short of excellence.

INTEGRITY We deal with our customers and colleagues ethically. We communicate openly and keep our promises. We practise professional integrity.

RESPECT We respect the value and contribution of each individual. We recognise and celebrate one another's success. We support one another's personal and professional growth to their full potential.

INNOVATION We take the initiative to innovate. We dare to dream and experiment even though it means taking risks. We forgive honest mistakes.

TEAMWORK We work across boundaries as a team to achieve our shared vision and goals. We make time to talk to each other and foster a strong sense of community within URA. We also work in partnership with the larger community outside URA.

---

30 years is a good time to look back - and ponder ahead.

Singapore's urban development has been etched by visionary planners who have served the nation for three decades. It is a blueprint of growth realised through judicious management of scarce resources, and simple hard work.

Today, the city stands as a modern, efficient, sophisticated city among global cities, but still the work goes on. There is much to do in evaluating, conserving, redeveloping, creating in this space we call home; to make it the ideal environment in which we can live, work and play.

A year into being 30,
we are still dreaming,
planning and building.

30 YEARS AGO, *looking into the future,*
a blueprint was all we had – for a city that
was built for tomorrow, based on the needs
of a challenging time where limitations
were larger than the possibilities.

BUT WE PREVAILED.

2

Work

3 . 4
Title: Peabody Essex Museum
Format: Logo and print collateral
Studio: Minelli, Inc.
Art Director: Margarita Barrios-Ponce
Designer: Stephen Rowe
Client: Peabody Essex Museum
Typefaces: Myriad, Bodoni

"Bodoni and Myriad were chosen
as a metaphoric transition from the
historical and established to the
modern and progressive."

3

4

13

Trade Gothic

Designed by Jackson Burke

Purpose

For newspapers, especially classified ads

History

Once an ideal font for newspapers, Trade Gothic is now primarily used in advertising and multimedia presentations. Its history can be directly traced back to German grotesque forms and the development of News Gothic by Morris Fuller Benton in 1908. Between 1948 and 1960, Linotype commissioned Jackson Burke to create a more readable and modern newspaper font, and Trade Gothic was born.

Sample

Trade Gothic Medium   40 pt

abcdefghijklmnopqrstuv
wxyzABCDEFGHIJKLMN
OPQRSTUVWXYZ
1234567890

Work

1
Title: *I Remember King Kong (The Boxer)*
Format: Book Cover
Studio: Orange Juice Design
Art Director: Garth Walker
Designer: Garth Walker
Illustrator: Garth Walker
Client: Jacana Publishing
Typefaces: Trade Gothic, Handlettering

Garth Walker writes, "I have simply always liked Trade Gothic..."

2
Title: Anni Kuan Brochure
Format: Print brochure
Studio: Sagmeister
Art Director: Stefan Sagmeister
Designers: Matthias Ernstberger,
Eva Hueckman
Photography: Matthias Ernstberger
Client: Anni Kuan
Typeface: Trade Gothic

2

1

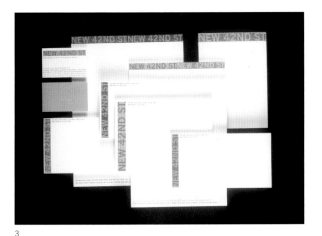

3

3
Title: New 42nd Street
Format: Corporate identity
Studio: Pentagram
Art Director: Paula Scher
Designer: Paula Scher
Client: New 42nd Street
Typeface: Trade Gothic

4
Title: Surfrider Foundation State of the
Beach 2003
Format: Annual report
Designers: Todd Houlette, Julie
Freeman, Mitch Morse
Client: Surfrider Foundation
Typeface: Trade Gothic

the islands: hawaii
and puerto rico. tropical
sandy beaches, coral
reefs and lush vegetation.

hawaii

puerto rico

37

hawaii

puerto rico

the mid-atlantic: new jersey's sandy
but hardened coast, the sandy barrier beaches
and dunes of the chesapeake bay
states—delaware, maryland and virginia.

new jersey

delaware

maryland

virginia

4

Work

5
Title: *Apocalypse*
Format: Poster
Studio: Why Not Associates
Art Director: Why Not Associates
Designer: Why Not Associates
Photographer: Tim Kiusalaas
Client: Royal Academy of Arts
Typeface: Trade Gothic

Trade Gothic was used because "we wanted a font that might appear on warning signs but that also worked well without the counters."

6
Title: *Nike Heroes*
Format: Film
Studio: Why Not Associates
Art Director: Why Not Associates
Designer: Why Not Associates
Client: Nike EMEA
Typeface: Trade Gothic

"We chose Trade Gothic because it looked good!"

6

5

7

7
Title: Holiday Bag
Format: Shopping bag
Studio: Todd Waterbury
Designer: Todd Waterbury
Illustrator: Todd Waterbury
Client: Bloomingdale's
Typeface: Trade Gothic

"The collage, made from a variety of international newspapers, required contrast from the serif fonts found on the newsprint. Trade Gothic provided contrast in legibility and form."

8
Title: LOOS Collateral
Format: Promotional folder
Studio: LUST
Designer: LUST
Client: LOOS Ensemble
Typeface: Trade Gothic

"Trade Gothic had a good combination of legibility and space conversation. We liked its look—conservative but not too bookish."

8

Univers

Designed by Adrian Frutiger

Purpose

For packaging, signage, and textbooks

History

Revolutionary in its design and form, Univers is a family of twenty-one typestyles designed by Adrian Frutiger. Its weight, proportion, and angle are all orchestrated in a unified family that is distinguished by numbers. Univers 55 is the parent face, the basis from which each variation was developed. Thus, all twenty-one faces can be used together in various ways. The design of Univers sparked a trend in type design toward a larger x-height.

Sample

Univers 55 Roman   40 pt

abcdefghijklmnopqrst
uvwxyzABCDEFGHIJKL
MNOPQRSTUVWXYZ
1234567890

Work

1
Title: *Art Work*
Format: Book
Studio: Art Center College of Design,
Design Office
Creative Director: Stuart Frolick
Designer: Rebeca Méndez, RMCD
Photographers: Various photography
students at Art Center
Client: Art Center College of Design
Typeface: Univers Extended

"Univers has one of the largest
font families, and in order to convey
a sense of stability and order, using
one family in a versatile way was
appropriate for the theme of
the book."

2
Title: *Ray Gun*, David Bowie
Format: Magazine article
Art Director: Chris Ashworth
Designer: Chris Ashworth
Client: *Ray Gun* magazine
Typeface: Univers

1

2

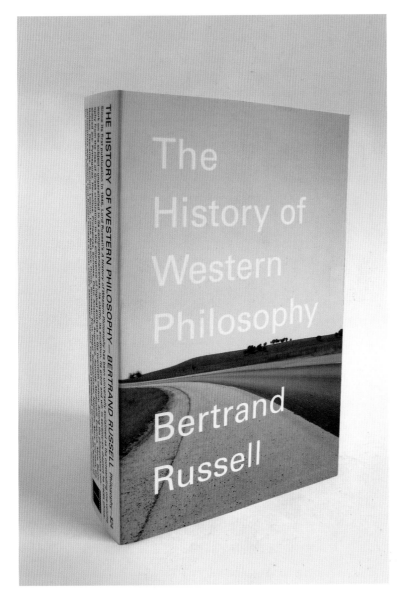

3

3 . 4
Title: *The History of Western Philosophy*
Format: Book cover
Studio: O.O.P.S.
Creative Director: John Fulbrook
Art Director: Paul Sahre
Designer: Paul Sahre
Photographer: Jason Fulford
Client: Touchtone
Typeface: Univers

"Univers = authority."

5
Title: Chatsworth Cemetery
Durban (Dartboard)
Format: Headstone (as found)
Photographer: Garth Walker
Client: Orange Juice Design
Typeface: Univers

Walker collects lettering samples from headstones throughout South Africa. Each family selects the font it wants from what is available at the burial parlor. This is a relatively new practice, a break from the traditional Western burial symbolism.

4

5

Work

6
Title: *It's How You Play the Game*
Format: Book cover
Studio: O.O.P.S.
Creative Director: John Fulbrook
Art Director: Paul Sahre
Designer: Paul Sahre
Photographer: Michael Northrup
Client: Scribner
Typeface: Univers

"The use of Univers in this case
allows the squares to be less
suggestive and less literal, as I don't
think I've ever seen Univers used
on a gameboard."

7
Title: Dysfunction
Format: Poster
Studio: Piper Design Co.
Art Director: Brian Piper
Designer: Eric Holman
Photographer: Matthew Cazier
Client: Lingo Dance Theater
Typeface: Univers

8
Title: *American Photography 19*
Format: Book
Studio: O.O.P.S.
Art Director: Paul Sahre
Designers: Tamara Shopsin,
Paul Sahre
Client: Amilus
Typeface: Univers

"The strict design system we used
for the book called for a typeface
that wouldn't call too much attention
to itself."

6

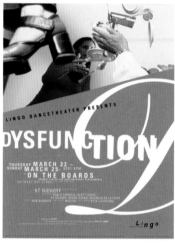

7

8

9

Title: *Soon: Brands of Tomorrow*
Format: Book spread
Studio: Chris Ashworth
Art Director: Chris Ashworth
Designer: Chris Ashworth
Client: Laurence King Publishing
Typeface: Univers

10

Title: Open
Format: Corporate identity
Studio: Open
Art Director: Scott Stowell
Designer: Susan Barber
Photographers: Cara Brower, Jenny
Carrow, Zak Jensen
Client: Open
Typeface: Univers

Open
180 Varick Street, no. 822
New York NY 10014 USA
+1 212 645 5633

www.notclosed.com

10

Work

11
Title: us≠u.s.
Format: Flyer/poster
Studio: Defacto Industries
Designer: Todd Houlette
Client: gw2004.us
Typeface: Univers

12
Title: Jazzfest Schaffhausen
Format: Poster
Designer: Ralph Schraivogel
Client: Jazzfest Schaffhausen
Typeface: Univers

13
Title: Art+Design Expo
Format: Poster
Studio: Kari Piippo Oy
Designer: Kari Piippo
Client: China Art+Design Expo
Typeface: Univers

11

12

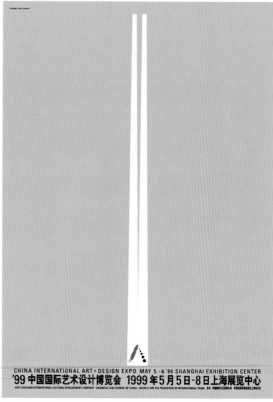

13

14
Title: Dentsu Head Office
Format: Signage
Studio: Kei Miyazaki/KMD
Designer: Kei Miyazaki/KMD
Client: Dentsu, Inc.
Typeface: Univers

"We used Univers because of its
simplicity and expression of an
advanced culture."

14

15

Vag Rounded

Designed by David Bristow, Gerry Barney, Ian Hay,
Kit Cooper, and Terence Griffin

Purpose

For instruction manuals and print advertising

History

Originally developed by a group of designers for Volkswagen AG (hence "VAG") in 1979, VAG Rounded is a variation on early nineteenth-century grotesque sans serif designs. VAG Rounded is unusual in that the terminal of every stroke is rounded. Adobe published an updated version of the font in 1989.

Sample

Vag Rounded Bold   40 pt

abcdefghijklmnopqrstu
vwxyzABCDEFGHIJKLM
NOPQRSTUVWXYZ
1234567890

Work

1
Title: Basel Prospectus
Format: Print publication
Studio: Form
Art Directors: Paula Benson, Paul West
Designers: Paula Benson, Claire Warner,
Paul West
Photographer: Kate Martin
Client: International School of Basel
Typeface: Vag Rounded

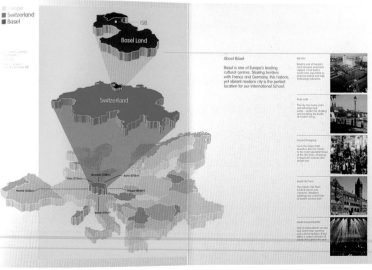

1

2

Title: Re:Creation entry form
Format: Print collateral
Studio: Form
Art Director: Paul West
Designers: Nick Hard, Paul West
Illustrator: Nick Hard
Client: Dazed & Confused, Topshop
Typeface: Vag Rounded Bold

3

Title: Q and Not U
Format: Poster
Studio: The Small Stakes
Art Director: Jason Munn
Designer: Jason Munn
Client: Q and Not U
Typefaces: Vag Rounded, Helvetica

"I used Vag Rounded to imitate the letters used in a stencil and simplified some of the letters to heighten that feel."

3

Work

4
Title: Tillskärarakademin 2002
Format: Annual report
Studio: Io
Art Director: Nathalie Barusta/ Io
Designer: Nathalie Barusta/ Io
Client: Tillskärarakademin
Typeface: Vag Rounded

5
Title: Tillskärarakademin 2004
Format: Annual report
Studio: Io
Art Director: Nathalie Barusta/ Io
Designer: Nathalie Barusta/ Io
Client: Tillskärarakademin
Typeface: Vag Rounded

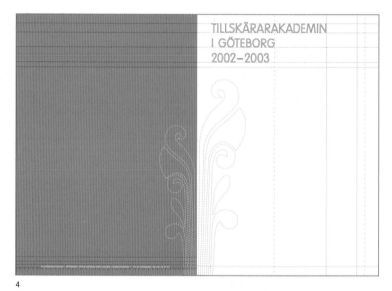

4

5

6

6
Title: Special Olympics Australia
Format: Print advertising
Studio: emeryfrost
Art Director: Vince Frost
Designers: Vince Frost, Clinton Duncan,
Prema Weir
Client: Special Olympics Australia
Typeface: Vag Rounded

"Vag Rounded was chosen because it is
a friendly, approachable typeface that
portrays an inclusive and youthful image
for the organization."

7
Title: Digital Depot
Format: Interactive kiosk
Studio: LUST
Art Director: LUST
Designer: LUST
Client: Museum Boijmans van Beuningen,
Rotterdam
Typeface: Vag Rounded

"Because of the way the images and text
are 'projected' onto the screens, a font
was needed that was 'sturdy' and yet very
legible... After many tests, Vag Rounded
was the most legible and beautiful font."

7

16

Adobe Caslon

Designed by Carol Twombly

Purpose

For magazines, journals, textbooks, and corporate communication

History

The Caslon legacy began in 1725 with the founding of the Caslon Type Foundry in England by William Caslon I, and lasted for three generations. In 1734, Caslon's first one-page specimen was produced, illustrating forty-seven of his typefaces, including Caslon. Based on seventeenth-century Dutch old-style designs, the Caslon font was popular throughout Europe and spread to the American colonies. Caslon was even chosen as the typeface for the first printing of the American Declaration of Independence and the U.S. Constitution. In 1990, designer Carol Twombly used the specimen pages of the late Caslon to update the font.

Sample

Adobe Caslon Regular   40 pt

abcdefghijklmnopqrstuv
wxyz ABCDEFGHIJKL
MNOPQRSTUVWXYZ
1234567890

Work

1

Title: *Arcade Magazine* 18.4:
"Architecture and Design
in the Northwest"
Format: Magazine
Studio: Piper Design Co.
Art Director: Christina Stein
Designers: Christina Stein,
Brian Piper
Client: *Arcade Magazine*
Typefaces: Futura, Caslon 224

"Throughout the publication we
used a strict grid of 'slightly rounded
connecting segments' and Futura —
with its varying weights and 'Bauhaus'
feel — was a nice complement to
this. We used it for headlines, section
titling (set in caps) and for very large
pull quotes. Caslon 224 was
chosen for body text for its easy
readability; it was also a nice classical
contrast to Futura."

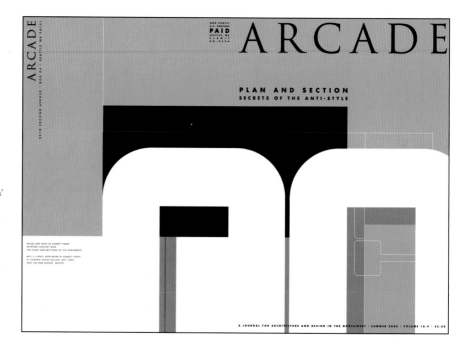

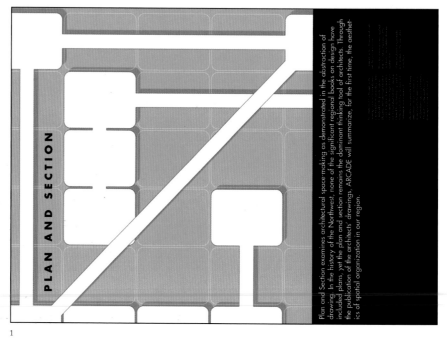

1

Title: LOOS Speed Music Festival
Format: Poster and program
Studio: LUST
Art Director: LUST
Designer: LUST
Client: LOOS Ensemble
(the Hague)
Typeface: Adobe Caslon

"Caslon was used to give the
otherwise heavily 'digital' nature of
the image a 'literary' and
'cultural' feel."

Work

3 . 4
Title: *Typographic 60*
Format: Print publication
Studio: A2 Graphics/SW/HK
Art Directors: Scott Williams,
Henrik Kubel
Designers: Scott Williams,
Henrik Kubel
Photographers: Various
Client: International Society of
Typographic Designers (ISTD)
Typeface: Woodtype and metal
Caslon, custom-made type

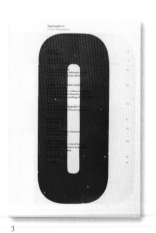

Hairspace
A thin piece of metal used for refined spacing of type, particularly capitals, and varying in thickness.

Imposition
The arrangement of pages of type so that pages which are to be printed together within a forme will be in the correct sequence when the sheet is folded.

Indenture
A formal contract of apprenticeship.

Monotype
Type cast as individual characters. The composition system comprises a spool-controlled mechanical typesetting/typecasting machine (pictured page 8) and a special keyboard to generate the central spool.

Same lijn as 2 6pt. The Monotype Supercaster casts individual type characters sizes from 5pt up to 72pt, for composing by hand.

Quoin
A wedge made of wood or metal, or a mechanically expanding metal block, used to lock type and furniture into a forme.

LONG PRIMER SMALL PICA

10

11

A deeper interest in Arabic books developed in Rome, where Duke Ferdinand I established a printing press for the Medici family. At Duke Ferdinand's request, the French type designer Robert Granjon was asked to design distinguished Arabic letters. Granjon engraved four Arabic character-sets, four sizes, for the Medici press and published several luxurious books including *The Sacred Evangelists*, beautifully illustrated by Tempesta.

Another famous printing press in Italy was one owned by François Savary de Brèves, French ambassador to the Ottoman Sultan and a passionate enthusiast for Oriental cultures. In addition to those cut by Granjon for the Medici printing house, more fascinating Arabic letters were engraved in Paris by François Savary de Brèves and brought to Rome, where he printed several religious books; among them *The Psalms* and *The Catechism* (Figure 1).

The establishment of Oriental printing presses consecutively appearing in Europe were: the printing house 'Intishar al Iman' (Spread of the Faith, or Propaganda Fidei) in Rome; followed by specialised printing presses in Leyden in Holland; the Imprimerie Royale in France; and later still, London and Oxford printing presses in England. In addition, it is also important to mention the contribution of the following European cities in the editing and publishing of Oriental languages: Venice, Milan, Padua, Uppsala, Leipzig, Frankfurt, Copenhagen and Palermo.

Arabic Printing in Constantinople and Syria
The establishment of printing in Constantinople was regarded with suspicion at first by the Ottoman Sultans for fear of its impact on their manuscript Koranic codexes and other religious texts. The first printing house was founded in Constantinople by a Jewish scientist who came to the Levant at the end of the 15th century to publish religious books using Hebrew typefaces. Arabic texts were also published in this press but using only the Hebrew typeface. The first printed book to appear in Arabic was *Kitab Tahrir Ousul al Handasa li Uqlidis*, published by Al Tusi (Euclid's *elementorum geometricorum*) in the year 1801 (Figure 2).

Spreading to the neighbouring countries at the beginning of the 17th century, printing entered Syria and a press was established in the monastery of Saint Antoine of Koushayya, in the North Lebanon Mountains. We only know one of the titles printed by this press: *The Psalms*, in the year 1610. This book was set in two columns and printed bilingually in Arabic and Syriac, the cult language of the Maronite (Christian) rite. This printing press resumed its function at the beginning of the 19th century, using both Syriac and Garsuni typefaces.

The appearance of the Arabic typeface occurred in the first decade of the 18th century at the city of Aleppo, Syria. In his book, *Arabic Publications*, the scientist Schnurrer considered these typefaces to be imported from the city of Bucharest, Roumania, while the

Figure 1
Title page of the Book of Psalms, printed by Savary de Brèves in Rome, Italy.

Figure 2
The first printed book to appear in Arabic: 'Tahrir Ousul al Handasa li Uqlidis', by Al Tusi (Euclid's Elementorum geometricorum libri tredecim).

Figure 3
The title page of 'Kitāb Al Zabūr' (the book of Psalms) printed by Pierre Forone in Nicolas Glisemhard's printing house, Italy.

54

55

4

17

Adobe Garamond

Designed by Robert Slimbach

Purpose

For textbooks and magazines

History

While sixteenth-century printer/publisher Claude Garamond (1480-1561) is often credited with the design of the original Garamond, the work of Jean Jannon (1580-1635) may also have been key in its development. A typeface based on the work of Jannon was introduced at the Paris World's Fair in 1900 as "Original Garamond." This event incited many type foundries to cast similar faces, sparking a renewed interest in the re-creation of Garamond that continued throughout the twentieth century. In the early 1990s, Adobe commissioned Robert Slimbach to redesign the font and Adobe Garamond was born.

Sample

Adobe Garamond Regular 40 pt

abcdefghijklmnopqrstuvw
xyzABCDEFGHIJKLMN
OPQRSTUVWXYZ
1234567890

Work

1
Title: *The Indexical Archive:*
The 21st Annual 100 Show of Excellence
Format: Book cover
Studio: Walker Art Center
Art Director: Andrew Blauvelt
Designers: Andrew Blauvelt,
Santiago Piedrafita
Client: The American Center for Design
Typeface: Adobe Garamond

2
Title: *Double Vision: Insights 2003*
Format: Poster
Studio: Walker Art Center
Art Director: Andrew Blauvelt
Designers: Andrew Blauvelt, Kyle Blue
Photographer: Chad Kloepfer
Client: Walker Art Center, AIGA
Minnesota
Typeface: Adobe Garamond

2

1

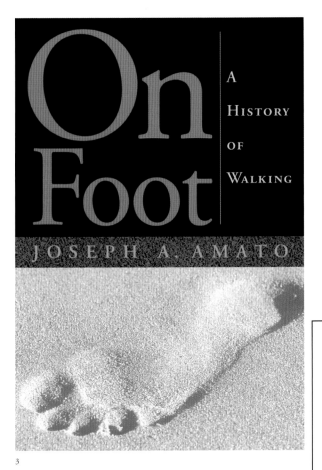

3

3

Title: *On Foot*
Format: Book cover
Studio: Worksight
Designer: Worksight
Client: NYU Press
Typeface: Adobe Garamond

"Claude Garamond's old-style typeface
reflects the history of the subject
coupled with the fact that it has a tall
x-height to fill the short title out
as a unit."

4

Title: Lip Service (Ravenna Marching
Band)/ *The Rocket*
Format: Newspaper page
Studio: Art Chantry Design Co.
Designer: Art Chantry
Photographer: Stephen Strickland
Client: *The Rocket*
Typefaces: Adobe Garamond (sidebar),
Times Roman (Body), Clarendon
(caption), Helvetica (title), Gill Sans
(initial caps), and a touch of Futura

4

Work

5
Title: Not again
Studio: Art Chantry Design Co.
Designer: Jamie Sheehan
Client: Peace Heathens/
Seattle Hempfest
Typefaces: Adobe Garamond, OCRB

6
Title: *Sphere* magazine
Format: Magazine cover
Studio: Worldstudio
Art Directors: Mark Randall,
David Sterling
Designer: Santiago Piedrafita
Editors: Peter Hall, Emmy Kondo
Client: Worldstudio Foundation,
Adobe Systems, Inc.
Typeface: Adobe Garamond

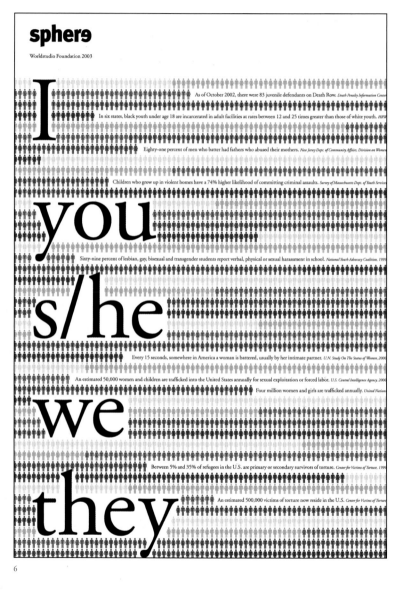

6

5

7

7
Title: iDeer
Format: Postcard
Studio: Citrus
Art Directors: Jim Cooper & Steve
Meades / Citrus
Designers: Jim Cooper & Steve
Meades / Citrus
Client: Citrus
Typefaces: Adobe Garamond,
Citrus custom bitmap font

8
Title: *Sphere* magazine
Format: Magazine spread
Studio: Worldstudio
Art Directors: Mark Randall,
David Sterling
Designer: Daniela Koenn
Editors: Peter Hall, Emmy Kondo
Client: Worldstudio Foundation,
Adobe Systems, Inc.
Typefaces: Adobe Garamond,
Akzidenz Grotesk

8

18

Bembo

Designed by Monotype Staff, Stanley Morison

Purpose

For posters, packaging, and textbooks

History

The earliest of the old-style typefaces, Bembo was inspired by
Classicist writer Pietro Bembo in 1496. The font was first developed
by Renaissance printer Aldus Manutius. He used a new weight of
a roman face to print Bembo's short piece "De Aetna." Bembo soon
evolved into the standard text type in Europe and was used this
way for over two hundred years. Later modified in 1929 by Stanley
Morison for the Monotype Corporation in London, Bembo is
a mature typeface with a rich history. It lends a classical feel
to any application.

Sample

Bembo Regular 40 pt

abcdefghijklmnopqrstuv
wxyzABCDEFGHIJKLM
NOPQRSTUVWXYZ
1234567890

Work

1
Title: Bembo Bomb
Format: Postcard
Studio: LSD
Art Directors: Sonia Diaz,
Gabriel Martinez
Designers: Sonia Diaz,
Gabriel Martinez
Client: LSDspace
Typeface: Bembo

From the same political postcard series
as Avenir Utopia and Times Sweet
Times, "Bembo Bomb represents
broken classicism. In this case, we used
the font to talk about terrorism. It was
an homage to victims of the Madrid
terrorist attack and of 9/11."

NEW YORK
MADRID
SEPTEMBER 2001 / MARCH 2004
Bembo / Bomb_11M   www.lsdspace.com

1

2 . 3
Title: Tai chi and Qigong school
Format: Print collateral
Studio: reinhardt (typo)grafisch
ontwerp
Art Director: Sabine Reinhardt
Designer: Sabine Reinhardt
Client: Tai chi & Qigong
school Balans
Typefaces: Bembo, Gill Sans

"The Old Face Bembo is both
elegant and architectural."

2

3

Work

4 . 5
Title: Next Directory 7
Format: Catalog
Studio: Why Not Associates
Art Director: Why Not Associates
Designer: Why Not Associates
Client: Next
Typefaces: Bembo, Gill Sans

"We wanted two very different fonts
that complemented each other. Hence
the choice of Bembo and Gill Sans."

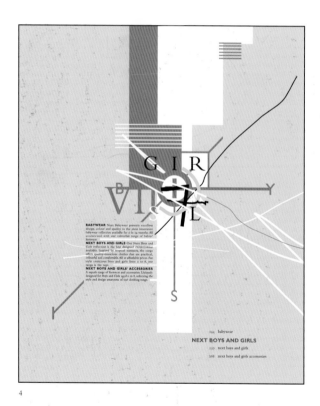

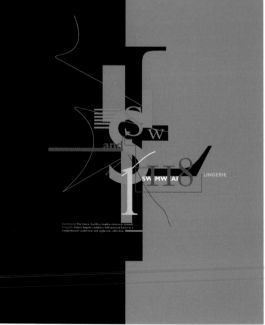

4

5

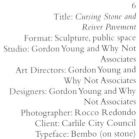

6

Title: *Cursing Stone and
Reiver Pavement*
Format: Sculpture, public space
Studio: Gordon Young and Why Not
Associates
Art Directors: Gordon Young and
Why Not Associates
Designers: Gordon Young and Why
Not Associates
Photographer: Rocco Redondo
Client: Carlile City Council
Typeface: Bembo (on stone)

"Bembo was chosen for the stone
to give it a sense of time."

6

19

Bodoni

Designed by Morris Fuller Benton

Purpose

For headlines, text, and logos

History

Developed by Giambattista Bodoni during the Classical period
(1760-1810), the original Bodoni is an elegant and precise font.
Strong characters, along with its thick and thin strokes, make it
an easily recognizable font. One of the most popular typefaces
until the mid-nineteenth century, Bodoni still inspires innovation.
A modern example, Bauer Bodoni, designed by Heinrich Jost in
1926 for the Bauer Font Foundry, features forms closely related
to the original but with even more delicacy. The version of
Bodoni in primary use today was created between 1908 and 1915
by Morris Fuller Benton for American Type Founders Company.

Sample

Bodoni Roman   40 pt

abcdefghijklmnopqrstu
vwxyzABCDEFGHIJKL
MNOPQRSTUVWXYZ
1234567890

Work

1
Title: Dali's Year Promotion
Format: Poster
Studio: Bis]
Art Director: Bis]
Designers: Àlex Gifreu, Pere Alvaro,
Carles Murillo, Jesús Novillo
Photographers: Various
Client: Gala-Salvador Dali's
Foundation
Typeface: Bodoni

"Bodoni was Dali's favorite type…
It is also one of our favorites.
It was a great coincidence."

2 . 3
Title: Peabody Essex Museum
Format: Print collateral, signage
Studio: Minelli, Inc.
Art Director: Margarita
Barrios-Ponce
Designer: Stephen Rowe
Client: Peabody Essex Museum
Typefaces: Bodoni, Myriad

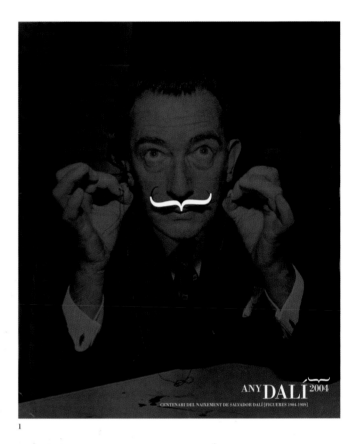

1

2

3

4

4 . 5 . 6
Title: The Kite-Eating Tree,
Method: Fail, Repeat ...
Format: CD packaging
Studio: Hydrafuse
Art Director: Greg Bernstein
Designer: Greg Bernstein
Photographer: Aaron Fitzgerald
Client: The Kite-Eating Tree
Typefaces: Bodoni Bold,
Stylograph, Berthold Akzidenz
Grotesk Medium Condensed Italic

5

6

Work

7
Title: *i-jusi* #11 (National
Typografika 1)
Format: Magazine cover
Studio: Orange Juice Design
Art Director: Garth Walker
Designer: Brandt Botes
Illustrator: Brandt Botes
Client: Orange Juice Design
Typeface: Bodoni

"Bodoni was chosen to represent
'classic Western typeface design'
— something African typography
certainly isn't!"

8
Title: Nuyorican Poets Café
Format: Poster and advertisement
Studio: Clare Ultimo Inc.
Art Director: Clare Ultimo
Designer: Clare Ultimo
Client: Nuyorican Poets Café
Typeface: Bodoni

"I didn't set out to mess up Bodoni,
but I wanted to use it because it
always feels literary to me. And
'distorting the classical' is what
poetry slam and spoken word
actually exist to do."

8

7

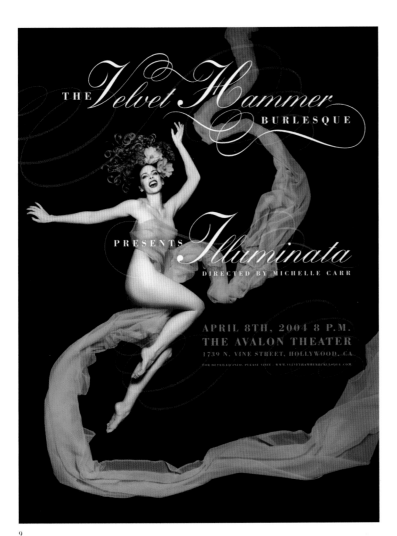

9

9
Title: The Velvet Hammer
Burlesque Illuminata
Format: Poster
Studio: SRG Design
Art Director: Steven R. Gilmore
Designer: Steven R. Gilmore
Photographer: Austin Young
Client: The Velvet Hammer
Burlesque
Typeface: Bodoni

"I wanted this poster to have
the look and feel of an old
champagne advertisement, and
Bodoni is a perfect typeface for
portraying a sense of
classic style."

10
Title: The Icarus Line
Format: Poster
Studio: Aesthetic Apparatus
Art Directors: Michael Byzewski,
Dan Ibarra
Designers: Michael Byzewski,
Dan Ibarra
Client: First Avenue and
7th St. Entry
Typeface: Bodoni

"Considering the name of the
band, we wanted to use a classic
serif face, but also wanted to
make sure it appeared to have
been chewed and spit out by
rabid vampire dogs."

10

20

Clarendon

Designed by Fann Street Foundry

Purpose

For dictionaries and headlines

History

The most revealing characteristic of Clarendon is its bracketed serifs, making it a striking contrast to typical serif designs. First issued in 1845 by the Fann St. Foundry in England, Clarendon has evolved through redesigns by Hermann Eidenbenz in 1953 and Albert Kapr in 1965 (creating Clarendon Antigua). Clarendon is still used frequently in dictionaries and headlines. With concise and enduring forms, Clarendon maintains a modern sensibility.

Sample

Clarendon Roman 40 pt

abcdefghijklmnopqrs
tuvwxyzABCDEFGH
IJKLMNOPQRSTUV
WXYZ
1234567890

Work

1

Title: Art Academy of Cincinnati
Format: Print publication
Studio: Automatic and Design
Art Director: Lori Siebert
Designers: Charles Wilkin,
Lori Siebert, Kirk Smith
Illustrators: AAC Students
Photographers: AAC Students
Client: Art Academy of Cincinnati
Typeface: Clarendon

2

Title: *The Desk Standard Dictionary*
Format: Book
Studio: Funk & Wagnalls Company
Typeface: Clarendon

Published in 1925, this document
shows Clarendon in its traditional
usage.

1

2

3

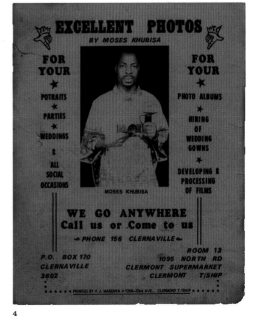

4

3
Title: Coil campaign
Format: Poster and CD packaging
Studio: Form
Art Director: Paul West
Designer: Nick Hard
Illlustrator: Nick Hard
Client: Imperial Records, Japan
Typeface: Clarendon

4
Title: *i-jusi* #19 (Foto issue),
"Excellent Photos"
Format: Magazine page
Studio: Orange Juice Design
Art Director: Garth Walker
Designer: Garth Walker
Photographer: Moses Khubisa
Client: Orange Juice Design
Typefaces: Clarendon, Futura

Work

5
Title: Bum cover (Front and Back)
Format: 7" record packaging
Studio: Art Chantry Design Co.
Art Director: Art Chantry
Designer: Art Chantry
Client: Lance Rock Records
Typefaces: Clarendon, Franklin
Gothic, Helvetica

6
Title: American Patrol
Format: Logo
Studio: Art Chantry Design Co.
Art Director: Art Chantry
Designer: Art Chantry
Client: Piccadilly Records
Typeface: Clarendon

7 . 8
Title: Malcom Morley exhibition
collateral
Format: Catalog
Studio: Base
Art Director: Base
Designer: Base
Client: Zavier Hufkens
Typeface: Clarendon

"We chose Clarendon in
consideration of Morley's work,
which we find to possess a certain
'roundness' and to be a bit naive."

5

7

6

8

9

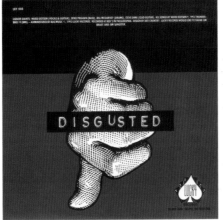

10

9
Title: Monkeywrench
Format: LP and 7"
record packaging
Studio: Art Chantry Design Co.
Art Director: Art Chantry
Designer: Art Chantry
Photographer: Charles Peterson
Client: Sub Pop Records
Typefaces: Clarendon, Futura

10
Title: Liquor Giants cover
(Front and Back)
Format: 7" record packaging
Studio: Art Chantry Design Co.
Art Director: Art Chantry
Designer: Art Chantry
Photographer: Charles Peterson
Client: Lucky Records
Typeface: Clarendon

Work

11 . 12
Title: D&AD *Ampersand*
Format: Magazine cover and spreads
Studio: Frost Design
Art Director: Vince Frost
Designer: Vince Frost
Photographer: Nadav Kander
Client: British Design and
Art Direction
Typeface: Clarendon

"Clarendon was chosen because it felt
right and worked well in the design of
the publication."

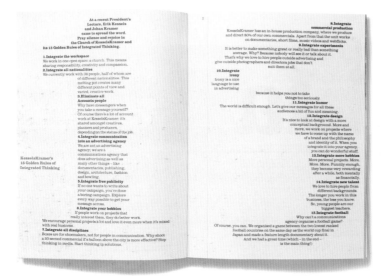

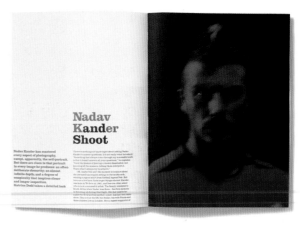

11

lead me on

Buckle Up

In Focus

D&AwarDs

Beam me

up

black

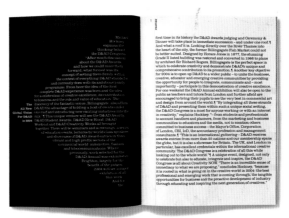

12

21

Courier

Designed by Howard Kettler

For tabular materials, technical documentation, and word processing

History

Though the typewriter is no longer synonymous
with office culture, the typewriter style
font Courier remains a viable typeface for
advertisments in the twenty-first century.
IBM first commissioned Howard Kettler to design
the face for use in typewriters in the 1950s.
The Hollywood standard for all screenplays,
Courier s digital version recollects the
vernacular of the era of the manual typewriter.
The font was also the U.S. State
Department s standard typeface until January
2004, when it was replaced with Times New Roman.
As a monospaced font, Courier has recently
found renewed use in the electronic world in
situations where columns of characters must be
consistently aligned.

Sample

Courier Medium   40 pt

abcdefghijklmnopqr
stuvwxyzABCDEFGHIJ
KLMNOPQRSTUVWXYZ
1234567890

Work

1

Title: ARTSWORD 2004
Format: Newsletter
Studio: Sommese Design
Art Director: Lanny Sommese
Designers: Anne Guillory,
John Heinrich
Photographers: Various
Client: Penn State School of
Visual Arts
Typeface: Courier

"Courier was selected to
give the piece a retro
newspaper feel— a reporter
just knocked it out on his
typewriter look."

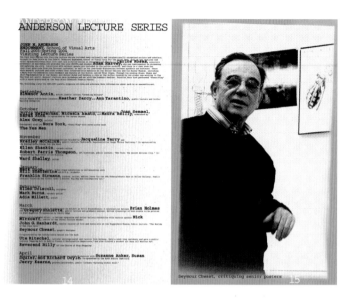

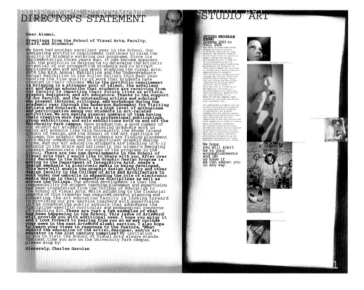

1

2

Title : Andreu Balius website
Format : Website
Studio : Andreu Balius
Art Director : Andreu Balius
Designer : Andreu Balius
Client : Andreu Balius
Typeface : Courier

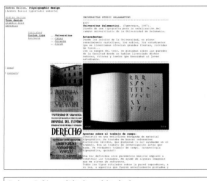

Andreu Balius, (tipo)graphic design
[Andreu Balius typestudio website]

Andreu Balius
Type design
Graphic work
Ephemera

Published
Custom type
Projects   ...Universitas
                ...Cañas
                ...Miranda
                ...**Forum**

[news]

[contact]

FORUM

ESP/
Tipografía FORUM
Diseño de una tipografía para la señalización del
Centro de convenciones. Barcelona, 2004.

Detalles:
Diseño basado en el módulo cuadrado.
(en colaboración con Mario Eskenazi)

ENG/
Typeface for the signal system at the International
Conference Center for Barcelona Forum 2004.
If you are interested in this work, please contact me.

© andreubalius
Barcelona, 2004

2

Work

3
Title: Labor Day Sale
Format: Poster
Studio: Todd Waterbury
Art Director: Todd Waterbury
Illustrator: Todd Waterbury
Photographer: Stanley Bach
Client: Bloomingdale s
Typeface: Courier

"Courier conveyed the
sensibility of news,
immediacy, and work."

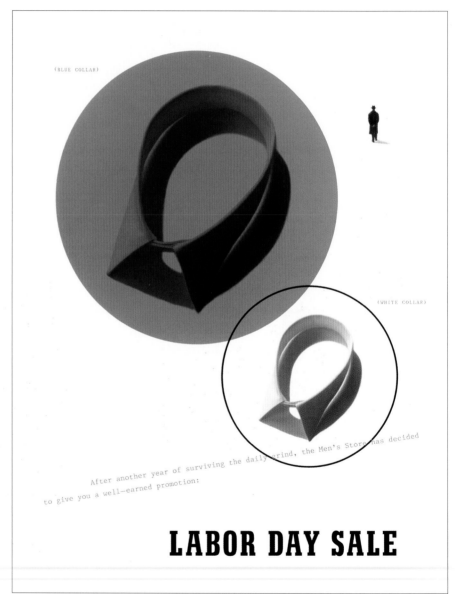

3

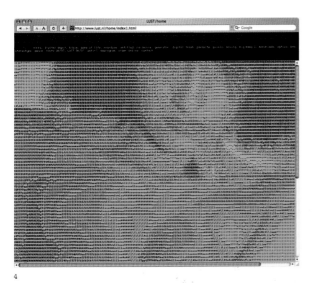

4

5

4.5
Title:LUST website
Format:Website
Studio:LUST
Art Director:LUST
Designer:LUST
Client:LUST
Typeface:Courier

"Of all the standard
monospaced web fonts, Courier
exhibited the best contrast
for ASCII art — something
I m sure the original designer
of the font didn t envision!"

6
Title:Home Base collateral
Format:Annual report
Studio:Anne Shackman Design
Art Director:Anne Shackman
Designer:Anne Shackman
Client:Home Base, Inc.
Typeface:Courier

"I chose Courier to reflect
the theme of drafting and
construction of a new company
direction."

t our core, we are a retail
company with the resources,
experience and vision to
continually evolve.

LEADERSHIP POSITION IN SOME OF THE
FASTEST GROWING SEGMENTS OF THE $160
BILLION HOME FURNISHINGS AND OUTDOOR
LIVING RETAIL SECTOR. A DEEP AS WELL
AS BROAD PRODUCT SELECTION WILL
POSITION THE NEW CONCEPT AS A DOMINANT
PLAYER IN KEY BUSINESSES WHILE, AT
THE SAME TIME, ADDRESSING A WIDE VARIETY
OF FOCAL POINTS THROUGHOUT THE ENTIRE
HOME - INSIDE AND OUT. IN ADDITION,
OUR SPECIAL EMPHASIS ON THE OUTDOOR
LIVING SEGMENT WILL CATER SPECIFICALLY
TO THE WESTERN LIFESTYLE, PROVIDING
US A CRITICAL POINT OF DIFFERENTIATION.

WE EXPECT TO TEST THE NEW CONCEPT IN
THE SECOND HALF OF THE CURRENT FISCAL
YEAR AT SELECTED STORES IN SEVERAL
MARKETS THAT ENCOMPASS A VARIETY OF
DEMOGRAPHIC, GEOGRAPHIC AND CLIMATIC
CONSIDERATIONS.

AT THE SAME TIME, WE REMAIN COMMITTED
TO SHORING UP MARKET SHARE IN THE
HOME IMPROVEMENT ARENA BY CONTINUING
MANY OF THE STRATEGIES WE EMPLOYED
LAST YEAR, WHILE MAKING NECESSARY
REFINEMENTS AND MODIFICATIONS TO KEEP
PACE WITH CONSUMER DEMAND.

WITH A BOOK VALUE OF OVER $10 PER
SHARE, HOMEBASE REMAINS IN SOLID
FINANCIAL STANDING, WITH A STRONG

BALANCE SHEET. AT JANUARY 29, 2000, THE
COMPANY HAD APPROXIMATELY $41.8 MILLION
IN CASH AND MARKETABLE SECURITIES,
OUTSTANDING CONVERTIBLE SUBORDINATED
DEBT OF $92.4 MILLION, $8.4 MILLION IN
CAPITAL LEASE DEBT AND STOCKHOLDERS'
EQUITY OF $395 MILLION.

DESPITE THE CHALLENGES WE ARE SURE TO
FACE THIS YEAR, WE LOOK FORWARD TO
PURSUING OUR LONG-TERM GROWTH OBJECTIVES.
IN THE END, SUCCESS WILL COME FROM OUR
ABILITY TO OVERCOME ADVERSITY IN PURSUIT
OF EXCITING NEW OPPORTUNITIES, RECOG-
NIZING THAT HARD-WON VICTORIES ARE THE
SWEETEST OF ALL.

ON BEHALF OF THE BOARD OF DIRECTORS
AND THE ENTIRE MANAGEMENT TEAM, WE EXTEND
THANKS TO OUR DEDICATED TEAM MEMBERS
TO WHOM THIS REPORT IS DEDICATED, AND
TO OUR VENDORS, CUSTOMERS AND STOCK-
HOLDERS FOR THEIR CONTINUED SUPPORT.

SINCERELY,

HERBERT J ZARKIN
CHAIRMAN, PRESIDENT AND
CHIEF EXECUTIVE OFFICER

6

22

Excelsior

Designed by Chauncey H. Griffith

Purpose

For newsletters, reports, and proposals

History

A newspaper typeface created in 1931 by Chauncey
H. Griffith of Linotype, Excelsior was one of the five
typefaces in Griffith's Legibility Group. The design of this
group of fonts was Griffith's direct response to advances
in newspaper production. Each font features an increased
x-height. These types were made specifically to be legible
even under the less-than-desirable printing conditions
that were inevitable in newspaper printing at the time.

Sample

Excelsior Roman   40 pt

abcdefghijklmnopqrs
tuvwxyzABCDEFGH
IJKLMNOPQRSTUV
WXYZ
1234567890

Work

1
Title: Kind of Like Spitting
Format: Record packaging
Studio: www.ianlynam.com
Designer: Ian Lynam
Illustrator: Ian Lynam
Client: Kind of Like Spitting
Typeface: Excelsior

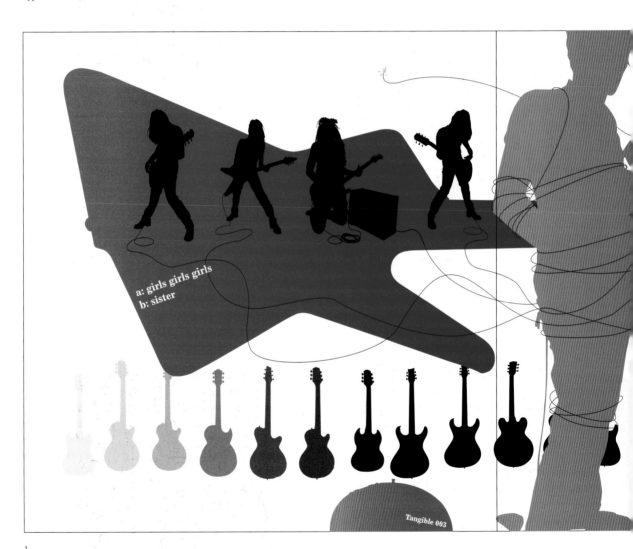

a: girls girls girls
b: sister

Tangible 003

1

kind
of like
spitting

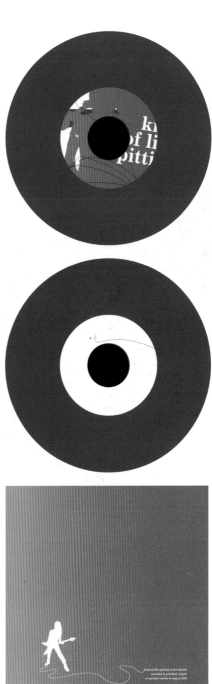

Work

2
Title: Excelsior Exploration
Format: Typographic experiment,
personal project
Studio: Defacto Industries
Designer: Todd Houlette
Client: Defacto Industries
Typeface: Excelsior

"What happens when the individual
letterforms of Excelsior are pushed
through repetition, cropping, color,
and transparency? At what point do
the letterforms become unrecognizable
and strictly illustrative? In the
process I focused on how much
a letterform could be simplified
and/or manipulated while
retaining its unique
characteristics."

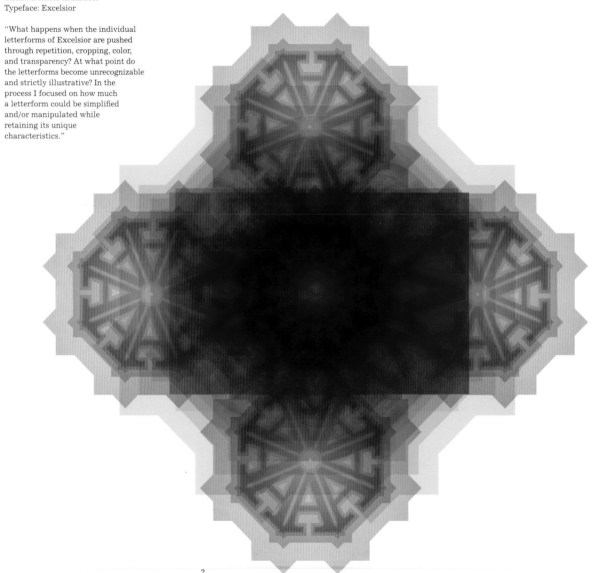

2

23

Lucida

Designed by Charles Bigelow, Kris Holmes

Purpose

For low-resolution printing, small point sizes, and reversed-out halftones

History

Built for bitmapped display screens and laser printing, Lucida was one of the first of the super family typefaces. Over fifty designs and variations of this font were created between 1984 and 1995 by Charles Bigelow and Kris Holmes of Bigelow & Holmes. Lucida is a sturdy font, ideal for difficult printing conditions and small point sizes.

Sample

Lucida Roman   40 pt

abcdefghijklmnopq
rstuvwxyzABCDEF
GHIJKLMNOPQRST
UVWXYZ
1234567890

Work

1
Title: *These Colors Don't Run*
Format: Monoprint
Studio: Joshua Berger Creative
Designer: Joshua Berger
Client: Portland Institute for
Contemporary Art (PICA)
Typeface: Lucida

A limited-edition monoprint for
Prints for PICA show.

2
Title: Malvar promotion
Format: Poster
Studio: www.ianlynam.com
Designer: Ian Lynam
Illustrator: Ian Lynam
Client: Third Row
Typeface: Lucida

1

2

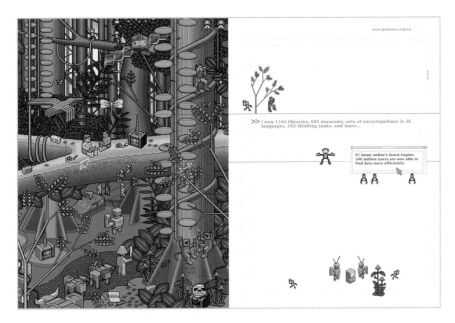

3
Title: PCHOME
Format: Print advertisement
Studio: Pao & Paws
Designer: Imin Pao
Illustrator: EBOY
Client: PCHOME
Typeface: Lucida

3

Work

4
Title: *2GQ* Issue #3
Format: Magazine
Art Director: Joshua Berger
Designer: Chad DeWilde
Client: *2 Gyrlz Quarterly*
Typefaces: Lucida, Embossed
Black Normal

QUEER & PLEASANT DANGER
The Kate Bornstein Interview
by Llewyn Máire & Lisa Newman

24

We recently performed at the 11th annual Performance Studies International conference at Brown University, alma mater of renowned transsexual writer, performer, and gender outlaw Kate Bornstein. Kate herself was kind enough to facilitate discussion with our audience and ask some tricky questions about what we had just done. We returned the favor after attending hyr brand spankin' new and absolutely genius solo performance, "Queer and Pleasant Danger."

The show is Kate's first fully theatrical solo performance piece since *Virtually Yours* in 1996. She describes the full-length two act piece as "a solo performance exploring through story, video, and a couple of songs, the comedy and tragedy of a sadomasochistic transsexual dyke inhabiting the simultaneous identities of daddy, daughter, father, and son as put into motion through a fundamentalist lens." An interview about this new work follows.

2GQ: *You asked us this question in reference to our performance at the conference, and now we'd like to ask you: How is "Queer and Pleasant" not reality TV? Where do the lines between performance art, theatre, and 'show biz' cross? Or do they?*

Kate Bornstein: Three things separate this new show from reality TV: it's not on TV, no TV station would ever air it, and it's scripted to within an inch of its life. But then again, don't we all script our lives all the time? Is it called art because we rehearse it first? We rehearse our scripts until we've got it as close to exactly the way we want our audiences to see us naked? Other than that, it might as well be reality TV, only more bloody and much, much cuter.

2GQ: *Though your writing and performances have been semi- and not-so-semi-autobiographical in the past, you've said that this performance is different from anything you've done before. Can you elaborate on that?*

KB: When I'm doing one of my college talks, I stand on a stage and I tell my story. It's part performance, part lecture—call it edu-tainment. But I've never direct-addressed a theater audience before, not as myself. I was trained in classical theater: Stanislavsky, Peter Brook, Chekhov, Shakespeare. It was all about playing a role written by someone else who was probably dead so you couldn't ask them what the character was all about. And you create a reality for that character that makes sense in the world of the play, but it's a character. It's not you... it's me. That's what theater meant to me.

Phoenix Festival

Adam Boshart has attended Phoenix Festival twice and was a co-founder of the Pot Luck theme camp. He is a married optician whose six-year-old daughter has been around electronic music all her life. Adam corresponded with Kerry Skemp about Phoenix.

Phoenix Festival describes itself as a weekend of "art, music, and mayhem created by the meeting of our minds with yours." The event thrives on participation from those who attend and is extremely receptive to new ideas, priding itself on its tradition of change. Festivalgoers buy tickets and camp out for the weekend, 90 minutes northeast of Portland in Trout Lake, Washington. Many stay for the weekend in theme camps—with names like ChickenHed, 1derland, Camp Puch, Pot Luck, and the Snausage Temple—based around creating art, playing music, or simply having an excellent time. The music at Phoenix Festival has included psychedelic trance, techno, house, breaks, drum & bass, and ambient sounds; performances include theatrical dancing and fire performance.

Phoenix Festival began in 2000, and during its first three years evolved in a cycle of life, death, and rebirth. After the end of this cycle, Phoenix Festival lay dormant for a year. In 2004, its organizers decided to bring it back by using the Asian version of the Phoenix myth. This year's festival will take place from July 21-25, 2005. Visit www.phoenixfest.com for more information.
—KS

How did you first get involved with Phoenix Festival?
The third Phoenix Fest [in 2002] was my first experience with the festival. I showed up with my wife Michelle, with no idea of what to expect. I brought along some of my records in hopes that someone would let me play on their sound system. After we set up our tent and camping area Michelle and I walked around the festival site. We had shown up early on the first day and were actually a little bored because there weren't many people and those that were there were busy setting up their stages and camps. We just went from soundstage to soundstage asking whoever looked like they were "in charge" of that area if we could help with anything. We were told "Thanks, but no," by almost everyone. However, one soundstage eagerly accepted our help. We worked with them to get their stuff set up and they were gracious enough to let me play records every evening of the festival. We were both really taken with their open-armed acceptance of us and have actually maintained a very close friendship with the people who set up that soundstage.

4

went through my gender change in 1986, and I came out the other side realizing that I was writing parts for trannies like me, and I still wanted to go onstage. Acting as a performance fix. But there was no playwright to blame if the character was unlikeable, or the script nonsensical, so more was on the line. But all my early pieces went through the veil of a made-up story. It was all metaphors. This show has a lot of metaphor, but it isn't a metaphor for anything. That's the big difference.

What role does the audience play in "Queer and Pleasant"? Are they witnesses? Messengers? Does their admission pay the bills? You ask the audience throughout the performance, can you see me? Am I real?" Do you expect a response, or is this merely a theatrical device?

The audience is the audience. They're all there for different reasons, aren't they? In all earlier shows, I'd cast the audience in their own part, usually something familiar enough to play along. I've cast audiences as talk show audiences, performance art audiences, and even as a computer-generated virtual audience. But in this show, it's really just me and you. I'm searching the audience for my daughter. Constantly. That's what makes contact with the audience so important. My daughter could be one of the audience. Maybe it's you?

2GQ: *You've spent several years deconstructing gender, gender presentation and identity. The roles/characters/avatars that you take on in this performance include your father, your own role as a father, and your past selves. You also address your fear of being perceived as clownlike. Because of these roles, you appeared more as a shape-shifter, a trickster, or a medium, rather than someone doing "drag." Can you talk about this?*

KB: Wow, cool. I had no idea how that would work out. You saw the very first ever performance outside my living room. So, I'm glad to hear the transformations worked. Before every show I do, I call in various spirits. One of these is Coyote, my sibling and most exalted trickster of them all. I call Coyote in to take over during the transformations. I do that before the show starts, and somehow s/he's there when I need hir.

2GQ: *Let's follow up that last question. Performing as a man is more than just going through the actions of putting on different clothes, shaving your head, or gluing on a moustache. How did you prepare yourself to revisit your experiences as a "man" or, more importantly, to embody the memory of your father?*

KB: I wrote from the part of me that's a 57 year old man. Let's face it, there's that part of me. I just haven't been living that part of me for nearly two decades, but finding that voice after all that time was surprisingly easy once I admitted it was there. And once I could write from that voice,

from a photo by Christopher Rainone

How has your involvement with Phoenix Festival changed over the years?
After our first festival, I wanted to do my own soundstage (or theme camp). I had an urge to do something other than just be there...I pooled the resources of many of my friends and we ended up doing our own theme camp last summer.

Can you describe your theme camp, both its appearance and any thoughts or "theory" behind it?
Our theme camp is called Pot Luck. That's the theory behind it. When you go to a pot luck, you bring whatever you have. Usually you bring your best dish for your friends and acquaintances to enjoy. Our camp has the same theory behind it—anybody can come and bring what they have to offer. We run a community kitchen where dinner is our best meal, and we provide a sound system with open turntables for anybody to come play records or CDs on. It doesn't matter what kind of music or skill level in playing music someone has, they can come play. It doesn't even matter if you don't bring any food for the kitchen. We have had and will have plenty to share. At the end of last year's festival, a couple of kids from Philly came up to our camp and gave us a blanket/tapestry that had a phoenix on it. Below the phoenix was the phrase, "neighbors caring for neighbors," and I think that sums up the spirit of what we do for our theme

camp. The people involved in setting up our camp compose of such a varied background I think Pot Luck describes the talent in the group too. There are an actress/dancer, two software engineers, a bio-chemical engineer, a civil engineer, two electrical engineers, a teacher, a CPA, etcetera. You get my point. Each person had something—their best dish so to speak—to bring to setting up the camp and each person did it so well last year.

What is your favorite aspect of Phoenix Festival?
I really liked the whole "do it yourself" aspect of the third year. That, in combination with the main stage, really blew me away. It's almost something you must experience, though, to fully grasp. It's pretty hard to put to words. At any rate, I really liked seeing the different characteristics of each person or group's efforts coming together into this crazy carnival of light and sound.

Anything else you'd like to say about Phoenix Festival?
If you haven't been yet, then go. It really has been a catalyst for helping change my outlook on life.

Minion

Designed by Robert Slimbach

For limited-edition books, newsletters, and packaging

History

A modern classic, Minion was designed by Robert Slimbach in 1990 for Adobe. Highly legible and beautiful, this font was inspired by late Renaissance faces. A gorgeous and utilitarian typeface, it couples both the simplicity of conventional text type with the complexity of digital technology. Suitable for a variety of uses, from special-edition books to newsletters to packaging, Minion is available in black weight, display, and swash fonts, as well as expert sets and a full range of ornaments.

Sample

Minion Regular   40 pt

abcdefghijklmnopqrstuv
wxyz ABCDEFGHIJKLM
NOPQRSTUVWXYZ
1234567890

Work

1 . 2

Title: Pioneers of Modernist Typography:
With or Without Feet
Format: Poster series
Studio: Pentagram
Designer: Angus Hyland
Design Assistant: Sharon Hwang
Clients: Pentagram, *Creative Review*,
AGFA Monotype
Typeface: Minion

"The serif type reflects the subtlety of
the portraits" in these four posters
depicting "pioneers of modernist
typography." The result is "a visual
language that conveys a sense of elegance
and modernism appropriate to each
poster's featured pioneer."

With or without feet: a series of talks about type
presented by Creative Review and sponsored by Agfa Monotype

New type design

Pentagram 11 Needham Road London W11 2RP Wednesday 19 February 2003 6.30 PM
tickets £10 students £7.50 email aminah.marshall@easteat.co.uk telephone Gavin Lucas 020 7970 6236
in association with Pentagram Design and Gavin Martin Associates

1

With or without feet: a series of talks about type
presented by Creative Review and sponsored by Agfa Monotype

Type on screen

Pentagram 11 Needham Road London W11 2RP Wednesday 14 May 2003 6.30 PM
tickets £10 students £7.50 email aminrah.marshall@centaur.co.uk telephone Gavin Lucas 020 7970 6256
in association with Pentagram Design and Gavin Martin Associates

Work

3
Title: Absecon
Format: Corporate identity
Studio: Worksight
Designer: Worksight
Client: Absecon Textile Mills
Typeface: Minion

"A revivalist font like Minion acknowledged the textile mill's tradition in craftsmanship, but the switch of a lowercase 'a' instead of a cap 'A' indicates that Absecon's fabric designs are not stuck in the past. The swirl symbolizes a bolt of fabric and a wave."

4
Title: Velocity Dance Center
Format: Poster
Studio: Piper Design Co.
Art Director: Brian Piper
Designer: Brian Piper
Client: Velocity Dance Center
Typefaces: Trade Gothic, Minion

"Trade Gothic accentuates modern dance's strengths, and Minion supports its classical roots."

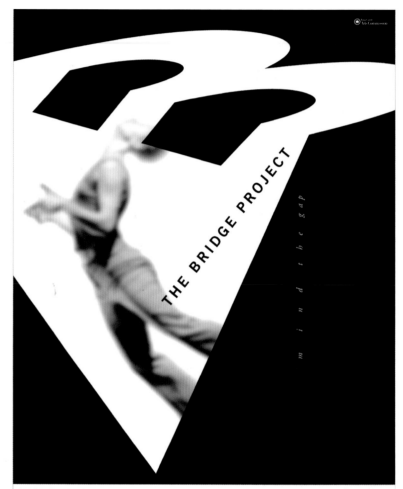

THE BRIDGE PROJECT

mind the gap

CHALIE LIVINGSTON / MAUREEN WHITING / AMY O'NEAL
JAN 25-27 2002 8:00PM AT THE VELOCITY MAINSPACE THEATER
TICKETS $12.00 WITH RESERVATION / $14.00 AT THE DOOR / $8.00 STUDENT RUSH 10 MIN. BEFORE CURTAIN
EACH NIGHT FOR RESERVATIONS / INFO CALL 206 325.8773 EXT. 2 WEB WWW.VELOCITYDANCECENTER.ORG
LOCATION 915 EAST PINE STREET 2ND FLOOR SEATTLE WASHINGTON 98122 CORNER OF PINE + 10TH AVENUE

velocity
DANCE CENTER

4

aBSECON

3

5

Title: Lingo Dance Theater website
Format: Website
Studio: Piper Design Co.
Art Director: Brian Piper
Designer: Eric Holman
Photographer: Matthew Cazier
Client: Lingo Dance Theater
Typefaces: Franklin Gothic, Minion

6 . 7

Title: Piper Design Co. promotions
Format: Posters
Studio: Piper Design Co.
Art Directors: Christina Stein, Brian Piper
Designers: Christina Stein, Brian Piper
Client: Piper Design Co.
Typefaces: Trade Gothic, Minion

"We chose Trade Gothic and Minion, two classic fonts that complement each other nicely and are our 'house' fonts."

5

6

7

25

Perpetua

Designed by Eric Gill

Purpose

For displays with fine lettering

History

Once claiming that typography was "not his country," Eric Gill later refuted this claim by creating his most successful roman typeface, Perpetua. As Gill was both a sculptor and type designer, it is no surprise that Perpetua has a chiseled look. Released between 1929 and 1930, Perpetua first appeared in the limited-edition book *The Passion of Perpetua and Felicity*. Today, the font still remains an excellent text typeface for long pages of text.

Sample

Perpetua Regular 40 pt

abcdefghijklmnopqrstuvwx
yzABCDEFGHIJKLMNOP
QRSTUVWXYZ
1234567890

Work

1
Title: *Predisposed #2*
Format: Art installation
Studio: RMCD
Art Director: Rebeca Méndez
Designer: Rebeca Méndez
Photographer: Rebeca Méndez
Client: Rebeca Méndez
Typeface: Perpetua

"Perpetua was appropriate for its classical,
academic personality."

2 . 3
Title: Art Center College of Design
recruitment collateral
Format: Catalog
Studio: Art Center College of Design,
Design Office
Creative Director: Stuart Frolick
Art Director: Rebeca Méndez
Designers: Rebeca Méndez, Darin
Bearman, Chris Haaga
Photographer: Steven A. Heller
Client: Art Center College
of Design
Typefaces: Perpetua, Minion,
Franklin Gothic

"If you are going to spend eight months
creating a design piece, might as well use
fonts you are completely in love with."

1

2   3

4

Title: A Flock of Words
Format: Public space
Studio: Why Not Associates
Art Director: Why Not Associates
Designer: Why Not Associates
Photographer: Rocco Redondo
Client: Lancaster City Council
Typefaces: Perpetua, Gill Sans

"The pavement points directly towards the magnificent art deco Midland Hotel, built in 1933. Much of the hotel interior was designed by Eric Gill. As homage to the great man, we only used his fonts in the design, including Gill Sans and Perpetua."

4

Work

5 . 6
Title: *Steelworks*
Format: Book
Studio: Why Not Associates
Art Director: Why Not Associates
Designer: Why Not Associates
Photographer: Julian Germain
Client: Whynot Books
Typefaces: Perpetua, Gill Sans

"The choice of the two fonts (modern
and classical) was to reflect the changes
the town of Consett had seen over the
past few decades."

5

6

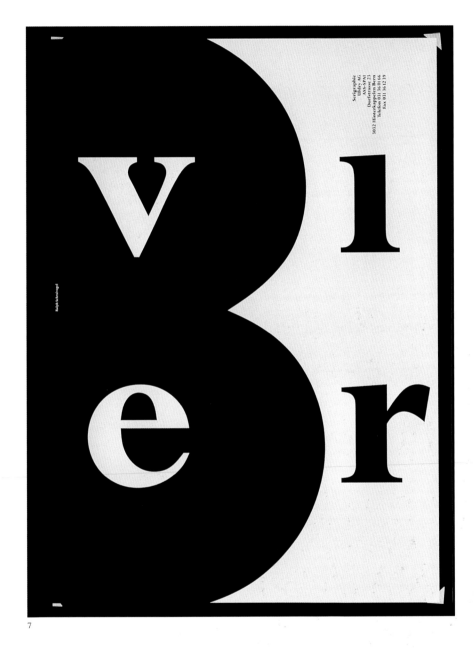

Title: B-four
Format: Silkscreened Poster
Designer: Ralph Schraivogel
Typeface: Perpetua

7

26

Sabon

Designed by Linotype Staff

Purpose

For books and corporate communication

History

The great Jan Tschichold named this type after French type-cutter and founder Jakob Sabon in honor of Sabon's typographic achievements. A descendent of early Claude Garamond faces, Sabon was jointly released by Stempel, Linotype, and Monotype foundries in 1967. Its achievement is as much in what cannot be seen as in what can. For the first time in history, a typeface that exhibited comparable quality whether used in manual casting, monotype, or line typesetting had been produced.

Sample

Sabon Roman   40 pt

abcdefghijklmnopqrstuv
wxyzABCDEFGHIJKL
MNOPQRSTUVWXYZ
1234567890

Work

1 . 2
Title: Scarlet, *Cult Classic*
Format: CD packaging
Studio: Asterik Studio
Art Directors: Don Clark, Ryan Clark
Designers: Don Clark, Ryan Clark
Client: Ferret Music
Typeface: Sabon

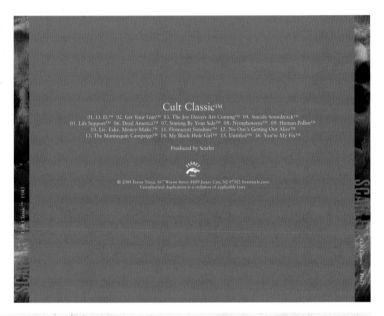

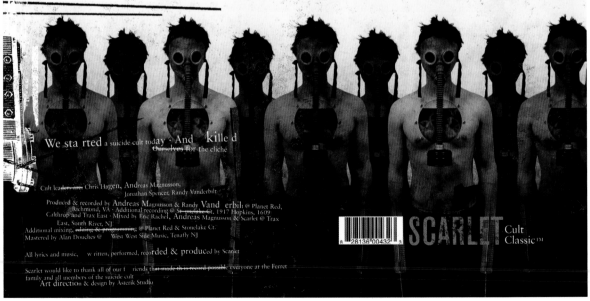

1

ONE

TWO

THREE

O.D.™

Welcome to the world of the manic depressed · Hopped up on Valium and in cardiac arrest · Hold me close · ...er when this world ends ·

We could share our endorphins · We could sleep with loaded shotguns and trigger happy ... The human pets neurotic and hopeless · We're all hopeless tonight · I don't need your therapy · I don't want your ...

Get Your Gun™

Johnny, get your gun · I'm not afraid to die · Johnny, get your gun · For a suicide pact tonight · Burning out with the Hollywood hopefuls · Johnny, I'm not your dying star · Ultra violence · Wrapped in cellophane

Bound and gagged in the back of my car · That cardboard cut was my swinging rope and skip ping toes · My world came crashing down

The Joy Decoys are Coming™

The joy decoys are coming · Dirty as a dollar and twice as numbing · Backstabbing salesmen telling you how to feel · Door to door gunpoint · They are making you kneel · The rip off artists are coming · Selling your flesh to the meat markets and running · Sleazy used car salesmen telling you how to feel · If you want love, you can buy love · Everyone is for sale · Your devil in a three-piece suit is here · his gun is Cocked to shoot ... who is fear · You are the money hungry prostitute swine · ... You are the money hungry prostitute swine · Open your legs and recite these lines

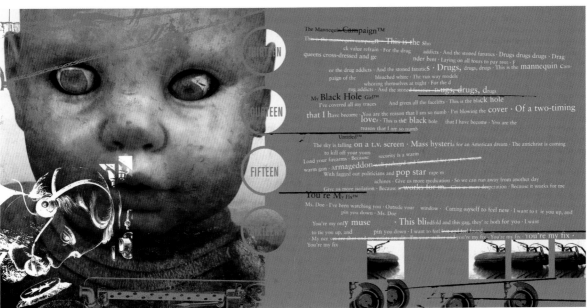

THIRTEEN

FOURTEEN

FIFTEEN

SIXTEEN

The Mannequin Campaign™

This is the mannequin campaign · This is the shock value refrain · For the drug addicts · And the stoned fanatics · Drugs drugs drugs · Drag queens cross-dressed and gender bent · Laying on all fours to pay rent · F...or the drug addicts · And the stoned fanatics · Drugs, drugs, drugs · This is the mannequin campaign of the bleached white · The run way models whoring themselves at night · For the drug addicts · And the stoned fanatics · Drugs, drugs, drugs

My Black Hole Girl™

I've covered all my traces · And given all the facelifts · This is the black hole that I have become · You are the reason that I am so numb · I'm blowing the cover · Of a two-timing lover · This is the black hole that I have become · You are the reason that I am so numb

Untitled™

The sky is falling on a t.v. screen · Mass hysteria for an American dream · The antichrist is coming to kill off your youth · Load your firearms · Because security is a warm warm gun · Armageddon ... · With fagged out politicians and pop star rape m...achines · Give us more medication · So we can run away from another day · Give us more isolation · Because it works for me · Give us more desperation · Because it works for me

You're My Fix™

Ms. Doe · I've been watching you · Outside your window · Cutting myself to feel new · I want to tie you up, and pin you down · Ms. Doe ·

You're my only muse · This blindfold and this gag, they're both for you · I want to tie you up, and pin you down · I want to feel ... · My nerv... and you're my fix · You're my fix · You're my fix · You're my fix

2

Work

3
Title: *The Procedure*
Format: Book cover
Studio: O.O.P.S.
Art Director: Paul Sahre
Designer: Paul Sahre
Dirt Cast Fist: James Croak
Client: Penguin Putnam
Typeface: Sabon

"I find myself using Garamond when I'm
designing the cover of a literary novel. For
this cover I wanted something Garamond-
like, without it being Garamond again,
for crying out loud."

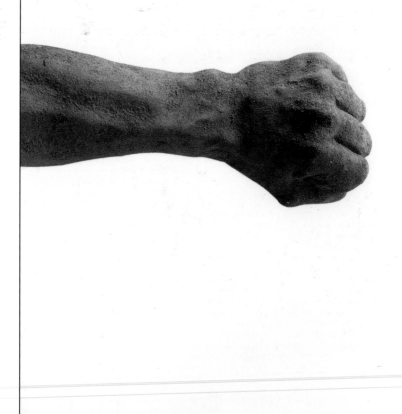

Harry Mulisch

THE PROCEDURE

A NOVEL BY THE AUTHOR OF *The Discovery of Heaven*

3

4

5

4
Title: *BEople*
Format: Magazine spread
Studio: Base
Art Director: Base
Designer: Base
Illustrators: Various
Photographers: Various
Client: Scoumont Publishing
Typefaces: Sabon, Helvetica

5
Title: *StillSuch*
Format: Book
Studio: Drenttel Doyle Partners
Creative Director: Stephen Doyle
Designer: Stephen Doyle
Photographer: Duane Michals
Client: William Drenttel New York,
Publisher
Typeface: Sabon

27

Stempel Schneidler

Designed by F. H. Ernst Schneidler

Purpose

For displays and fine, legible text type

History

Graced with charm and fine proportions, Stempel Schneidler was inspired by Venetian typefaces from the Renaissance. It was designed by F. H. Ernst Schneidler for the Bauer Foundry in 1936. It is a fine legible text type that is also useful for display type.

Sample

Stempel Schneidler Roman   40 pt

abcdefghijklmnopqrstu
vwxyzABCDEFGHIJKL
MNOPQRSTUVWXYZ
1234567890

Work

1 . 2
Title: PMI
Format: Print advertising
Studio: Pao & Paws
Art Director: Imin Pao
Designer: Imin Pao
Photographer: Imin Pao
Client: PMI
Typeface: Stempel Schneidler

PHOTOMAN
IMAGE.
LARGE PHOTO
OUTPUT.
2298.3368

1

PHOTOMAN
IMAGE.
LARGE PHOTO
OUTPUT.
2298.3368

2

Work

3
Title: NANYA 2005
Format: Calendar
Studio: Pao & Paws
Art Director: Imin Pao
Designer: Chih-Ling Wang
Illustration Artist: Casey Reas
Client: Nanya Technology Corporation
Typeface: Stempel Schneidler

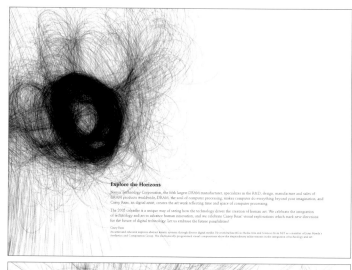

Explore the Horizons

Nanya Technology Corporation, the fifth largest DRAM manufacturer, specializes in the R&D, design, manufacture and sales of DRAM products worldwide, DRAM, the soul of computer processing, makes computer do everything beyond your imagination, and Casey Reas, an digital artist, creates the art work reflecting time and space of computer processing.

The 2005 calendar is a unique way of seeing how the technology drives the creation of human art. We celebrate the integration of technology and art to advance human innovation, and we celebrate Casey Reas' visual explorations which mark new directions for the future of digital technology. Let us embrace the future possibilities!

Casey Reas
An artist and educator explores abstract kinetic systems through diverse digital media. He received his MS in Media Arts and Sciences from MIT as a member of John Maeda's Aesthetics and Computation Group. His electronically-programmed visual compositions show the extraordinary achievements in the integration of technology and art.

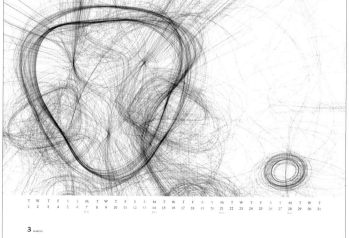

3 MARCH

3

4
Title: AS
Format: Print advertising
Studio: Pao & Paws
Art Director: Imin Pao
Designer: Imin Pao
Client: AS
Typeface: Stempel Schneidler

4

28

Times New Roman

Designed by Stanley Morison, Starling Burgess, and Victor Lardent

For newspapers, magazines, and corporate communication

History

A workhorse typeface, Times New Roman was designed in 1932 by Stanley Morison, a type consultant for the *Times* of London. "The new types for the *Times* will tend towards the 'modern,' though the body of the letter will be more or less old-face in appearance," he wrote in a memo to the *Times* committee. Morison achieved his goal — this modern newspaper face was the most successful type of its century and became ubiquitous in the next. It offers great contrast and is more condensed than typical newspaper fonts.

Sample

Times New Roman   40 pt

abcdefghijklmnopqrstuv
wxyzABCDEFGHIJKL
MNOPQRSTUVWXYZ
1234567890

Work

"I used Times in this case because I needed a typeface that would give the book 'portfolio-ness' as well as a contrast to the Helvetica that dominates the books."

1

2

3

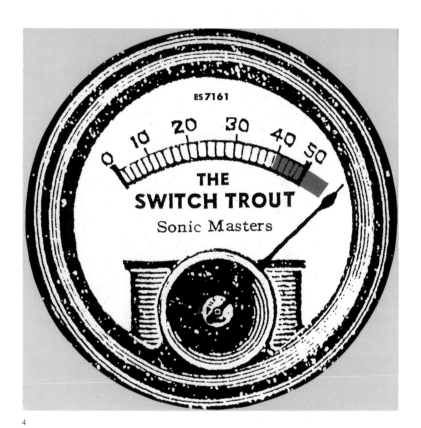

4

4

Title: The Switch Trout, *Sonic Masters*
Format: 7" record packaging
Studio: Art Chantry Design Co.
Designers: Art Chantry, Jamie Sheehan
Client: Dave Crider, Estrus records
Typefaces: Times New Roman, Futura

5

Title: *The History of Northwest Rock,* Vols. 1, 2, 3
Format: Record packaging
Studio: Art Chantry Design Co.
Designer: Art Chantry
Client: Jerden Records
Typefaces: Bembo, Bodoni, Caslon, Clarendon, Franklin Gothic, Futura, Garamond, Gill Sans, Perpetua, Sabon, Times New Roman, Trajan, Trade Gothic, Univers, and a few others

5

Work

6:
Title: Soundgarden/Pearl Jam, *The Rocket*
Format: Newspaper page
Studio: Art Chantry Design Co.
Designer: Art Chantry
Photographer: Lance Mercer
Client: *The Rocket*
Typefaces: Times New Roman,
Futura, Helvetica

7 . 8
Title: Times Sweet Times
Format: Postcard
Studio: LSD
Art Directors: Sonia Diaz, Gabriel Martinez
Designers: Sonia Diaz, Gabriel Martinez
Client: LSDspace
Typeface: Times New Roman

"This version of Times proposes to represent, through different grades of typographic erosion, the social aggression that some people suffer."

JEFF GILBERT CATCHES UP WITH CHRIS CORNELL AND EDDIE VEDDER AS THEY INCH THEIR WAY TO GLOBAL DOMINATION . . . . OR SOMETHING LIKE THAT

WHAT A LONG, STRAINED TRIP IT'S BEEN.

During the course of this musically tedious and tumultuous year, we've watched (with guarded patience) as two of our favorite homeboys, Soundgarden and Pearl Jam, inch their way toward global domination like big hairy slugs hot on the trail of rotting fruit. And, in the process, sell more records than a dead Elvis, swing their hair around on *Saturday Night Live*, and hang out with Axl. Seems you can't pick up a magazine anymore that doesn't have a fold-out shot of Chris Cornell's buff torso or Eddie Vedder hanging from a lighting rig.

It's been fun, really, this ringside seat. But through it all, Seattle's had to endure their success almost as much as they have. Let's face it, raging xenophobes that we are, it ain't easy sharing our bands and our beer at RKCNDY with the likes of *Rolling Stone* and *Entertainment Tonight* breathing down your face, just because you're wearing a Green River T-shirt, Doc Martens and might be in a band. The price of fame is indeed high.

This year, as the lofty price/prize of success, both Pearl Jam and Soundgarden are playing feature roles in Lollapalooza II, a *wunderfest* of politically correct music and politically correct politics — a Woodstock Lite for the '90s (same great bands, one-third less solos). As it was last year, the headline-making event (now relegated to Bremerton, the capitol of Alternative Rock) will feature all sorts of monstrously great bands (see *Rocket* calendar) and propaganda-spewing booths, dotting the concert site like ripe field mushrooms.

If the patently white funk of the Red Hot Chili Peppers doesn't move you to dance, or the mechanized syncopations of Ministry fail to realign your sense of reality, you'll still be able to do things like buy Made in Korea T-shirts printed with the *cause du jour*, publicly smoke pot without fear, resurrect the peace sign (still two fingers), and visit consciousness raising booths like *Rock The Vote*, where you can register to topple the government; or *Rock For Choice*, where you can sign up to take back the rights of your body; or the popular *Rock The Environment*, where you can learn to drink beer from an aluminum container outdoors without feeling guilty. Then there's one booth that's sure to be a hit — the *Rock The Grunge* booth, where you'll be able to sponsor a poor, outta state musician, and send him (or her) to Seattle to score a record deal. Ideally, Lollapalooza has something for everyone — especially if you're fans of Soundgarden and Pearl Jam. And we know you are.

Pearl Jam and Soundgarden are so famous now, we had to call half way around the world to talk to them. Chris Cornell had a cold and was hanging out, writing hits in his room at the Dusseldorf Ramada Inn (just a leiderhosen throw away from downtown Berlin); Guns 'N Roses have been dragging Soundgarden around Europe on tour. Eddie Vedder had just come off stage; Pearl Jam headlined a sold-out 50,000 seat festival in Hamburg. After doing a lengthy interview with a surfer magazine, he was still wide awake enough to chat with us. As usual, both singers had a lot to talk about and we had our tape recorder rolling (with fresh batteries) to catch every word. Not because they're stars now, but because it's always nice to hear from your friends. Even if they get to go to Germany and we don't. ▶ ▶ ▶ ▶ ▶

PHOTOGRAPHY BY LANCE MERCER

JULY 1992 : THE ROCKET 33

6

Times Sweet Times / www.lsdspace.com

7

LA TORTURA Y LOS MALOS TRATOS QUE SUFREN LAS MUJERES ESTÁ ENRAIZADA EN UNA CULTURA UNIVERSAL QUE NIEGA A ESTAS LA IGUALDAD DE DERECHOS CON LOS HOMBRES Y LEGITIMA LA APROPIACIÓN VIOLENTA DE SU CUERPO

Times Sweet Times / www.lsdspace.com

8

9

Title: DeProgram website
Format: Website
Studio: LUST
Art Director: LUST
Designer: LUST
Client: College for Creative Studies, Detroit
Typeface: Times New Roman

deProgram 2004.
info. participants. calendar. project1 :nlxl.
project2:lust. post-its.
project. day 1. day 2. day 3. summary.
MON, JULY 12

Iqbal
_____

Kristen

we all already have the ability to communicate our emotions non-verbally. The thing that needs to be done is for poeple to look at other people. We need to learn to be aware of other people out side of ourself. Study faces as they pass you by on the street and examine the emotions displayed. Stop looking down at the ground, stop not looking at other people. Maybe you will make eyeconact and you will experience a single momentary connection you may not have otherwise.

Laurent

My idea is that whatever is going on inside a person could be visible from the outside.

Livia

document stau= document traffic

how are we going to survive the document overload?
what do we understand under all those different codes.
what if our noses talk and our ears speak...
i am still exploring the effect of our extensions and their influence on us. we do not have to move anymore, because we can travel in the web. we can reach our friends through the web and we can buy, sell and pay things on the web.
we can play, research and even have sex on the web. we do not need to leave our house and it does not matter if i have a friend in buenos aires or in zurich, both of them are the same technological distance.

deProgram 2004.
info. participants. calendar. project1 :nlxl.
project2:lust post-its.
project. day 1. day 2. day 3. summary.
MON, JULY 19

Good Morning! Today you will have till 12.00 noon to finish up on your forays into the city, print out documentation, organize shot footage, etc.

At 12 we will meet at the Royal Academy to discuss your explorations and initial research.

Jeroen & Thomas

Some impressions of the 2nd day...

Iqbal
_____

Kristen

public space: streets, restaurants, parks, shops, schools, markets.

safety: day and night, clean or dirty area, well kept or run down, lots of people or no people, ...

began today by taking my map and marking the points of intersection made by the pre-existing grid. Rode to as many points as possible that were in a public space and made observations.

Laurent
So, I found out about the health care system, general information on the medical system as well, about current health issues (new

9

29

TRARIAN

DESIGNED BY CAROL TWOMBLY

FOR BOOKS, MAGAZINES, POSTERS, AND BILLBOARDS

HISTORY

THE MODELS FOR THIS ELEGANT AND CLASSICAL TYPEFACE ARE THE LETTERFORMS USED ON IMPERIAL TRIUMPHAL ARCHES (ARCH OF TITUS IN ROME, 81 A.D.) TO DOCUMENT CULTURAL EVENTS AND WARS. DESIGNED BY CAROL TWOMBLY FOR ADOBE IN 1989, TRAJAN IS A PURE VERSION OF THE FAMOUS ROMAN INCISED LETTER, WHICH WAS WRITTEN WITH A BRUSH BEFORE BEING CARVED INTO STONE. TRAJAN IS USED FOR DISPLAY WORK IN BOOKS, MAGAZINES, POSTERS, AND BILLBOARDS.

SAMPLE

TRAJAN REGULAR   40 PT

ABCDEFGHIJKLMN
OPQRSTUVWXYZ
1234567890

WORK

1
TITLE: BUILD — *PRINT WITH
LOVE* EXHIBITION
FORMAT: FLYER
STUDIO: BUILD
ART DIRECTOR: MICHAEL C.
PLACE
DESIGNER: MICHAEL C. PLACE
CLIENT: MAGMA, UK
TYPEFACE: TRAJAN (BUILD EDIT)

BUILD - PRINT WITH LOVE™
MICRO EXHIBITION
27TH AUGUST - 10TH OCTOBER 2004

MAGMA, 22 OLDHAM STREET, MANCHESTER
M1 1JN, UK
OPENING TIMES: 10 - 6.30 DAILY 11 - 5 SUNDAYS
T. 0161 2368777 - E: SIMON@MAGMABOOKS.COM
MAGMABOOKS.COM - DESIGNBYBUILD.COM

1

2

TITLE: *THE CONFERENCE OF
THE BIRDS*
FORMAT: BOOK COVER
STUDIO: DID GRAPHICS INC.
ART DIRECTOR: MAJID ABBASI
DESIGNER: MAJID ABBASI
PHOTOGRAPHER: IMAGE BANK
CLIENT: KHOJASTEH
PUBLICATION
TYPEFACES: TRAJAN. NASTALIQ
(PERSIAN CALLIGRAPHY)

"I FOUND TRAJAN VERY
SUITABLE FOR A CLASSIC.
ESPECIALLY WITH THE
NASTALIGH CALLIGRAPHY
IN PERSIAN."

2

WORK

3
TITLE: THOMAS KOHLMANN,
THE ANNUNCIATION
FORMAT: POSTER
STUDIO: PAONE DESIGN
DESIGNER: GREGORY PAONE
CLIENT: THOMAS KOHLMANN
TYPEFACE: TRAJAN

"TRAJAN WAS CHOSEN TO
REFLECT THE TRADITIONAL
RELIGIOUS THEME OF THE
PAINTING."

THE
ANNUN
CIA
TION

BY THOMAS KOHLMANN

A PAINTING FOR
SAINT THOMAS THE APOSTLE CHURCH
NEW YORK

ON VIEW IN
SAINT PATRICK HALL
TWENTIETH AND LOCUST STREETS
PHILADELPHIA

SUNDAY MARCH 28, 2004
9:00 AM – 3:00 PM

3

CHANNEL 39 WATCH WEATHER WATCH US.

4
TITLE: TV39
FORMAT: PRINT ADVERTISING
STUDIO: PAO & PAWS
ART DIRECTOR: IMIN PAO
DESIGNER: IMIN PAO
CLIENT: TV39
TYPEFACE: TRAJAN

4

30

Walbaum

Designed by Carol Twombly

Purpose

For magazines, journals, textbooks, and corporate communication

History

Dubbed the most beautiful specimen of German Modern Face, Justus Erich Walbaum's design is not only attractive, but also versatile. Ranked as one of the great European Romantic designers, J. E. Walbaum cut the type at Goslar and Weimar early in the nineteenth century. The typeface resembles aspects of Bodoni and Didot in its clear structure and simple forms.

Sample

Walbaum Regular   40 pt

a b c d e f g h i j k l m n o p
q r s t u v w x y z A B C D E F
G H I J K L M N O P Q R S T U
V W X Y Z
1234567890

Work

1
Title: Chou Hwei, *Where_3 Lonely City*
Format: Record packaging
Studio: Pao & Paws
Art Director: Imin Pao
Designer: Imin Pao
Illustration Artist: Thomas Barwick
Client: Linfair Records Limited
Typeface: Walbaum

2 .
Title: *The Political Problem of Luck*
Format: Magazine spreads
Studio: Plazm
Art Director: Joshua Berger
Designer: Tommy Kwak,
The/Open/Spaces
Photographer: Tommy Kwak,
The/Open/Spaces
Client: *Plazm* magazine
Typefaces: Walbaum, Mrs. Eaves,
Handwriting

Where_3
寂寞城市

Where Chu Image Campaign

1

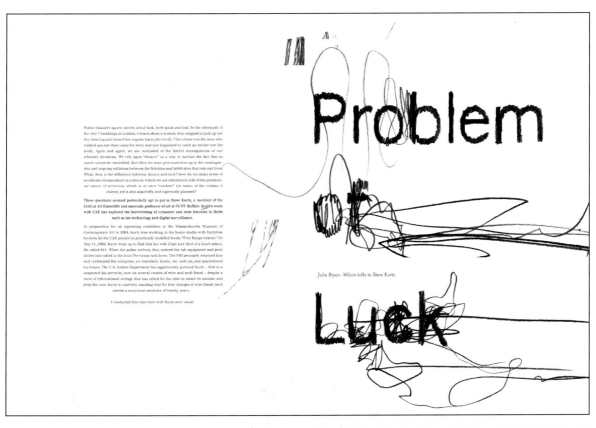

Public disasters spawn stories about luck, both good and bad. In the aftermath of the July 7 bombings in London, I heard about a woman who stopped to pick up her dry cleaning and missed her regular train (she lived). Then there was the man who walked quicker than usual for work and just happened to catch an earlier one (he died). Again and again, we are reminded of the fateful consequences of our arbitrary decisions. We rely upon "chance" as a way to narrate the fact that so much cannot be controlled, that often we must give ourselves up to the contingencies and ongoing collisions between the felicities and infelicities that rule our lives. What, then, is the difference between chance and luck? How do we make sense of accidental circumstance in a time in which we are relentlessly told of the paradoxical nature of terrorism, which is at once "random" (in terms of the victims it claims) yet is also assuredly and rigorously planned?

These questions seemed particularly apt to put to Steve Kurtz, a member of the Critical Art Ensemble and associate professor of art at SUNY Buffalo. Kurtz's work with CAE has explored the intertwining of corporate and state interests in fields such as bio-technology and digital surveillance.

In preparation for an upcoming exhibition at the Massachusetts Museum of Contemporary Art in 2004, Kurtz was working in his home studio with harmless bacteria for the CAE project on genetically modified foods, "Free Range Grains." On May 11, 2004, Kurtz woke up to find that his wife Hope had died of a heart attack. He called 911. When the police arrived, they noticed the lab equipment and petri dishes and called in the Joint Terrorism task force. The FBI promptly detained him and confiscated his computer, art materials, books, car, and cat, and quarantined his house. The U.S. Justice Department has aggressively pursued Kurtz – first as a suspected bio-terrorist, now on several counts of wire and mail fraud – despite a wave of international outrage that has called for the state to admit its mistake and drop the case. Kurtz is currently standing trial for four charges of wire fraud; each carries a maximum sentence of twenty years.

I conducted this interview with Kurtz over email.

Julia Bryan-Wilson talks to Steve Kurtz

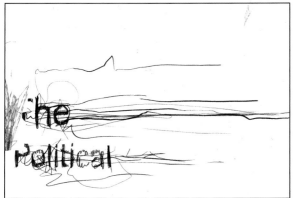

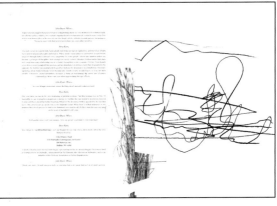

2

Work

3 . 4
Title: Golden Arrow
Format: Brochure
Studio: Pao & Paws
Art Director: Imin Pao
Designer: Tzuchan Shen
Client: Golden Arrow
Typeface: Walbaum

3

4

5
Title: Sony Playstation 2
Format: Print advertising
Studio: Pao & Paws
Art Director: Imin Pao
Designer: Imin Pao
Client: Sony
Typeface: Walbaum

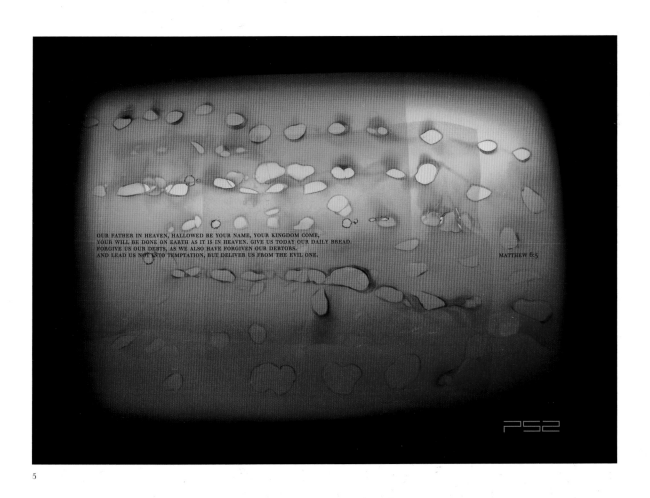

5

ALL 30

Designed by Ian Lynam

As students of typography we monitor the effects of letterforms on ourselves every day. And as visual communicators, we are arbiters of these typographic signifiers on friends, neighbors, and our culture at large. Subtle shifts in the principles of our mutually agreed-upon graphic language have the power to alter the reality of our surroundings. One only needs to glancingly review the evolution of letterforms from calligraphic strokes to black letters to serif and sans to understand how typography is reflected and refracted in our world. Ian Lynam proposed the following experiment as part of this book: Combine all thirty typefaces featured in this book into one font.

— The Editors

I wondered what would happen if a hybrid typeface were forged by interloping all thirty of the essential typefaces into one. I was curious if there were some underlying structural discoveries that would be revealed along the way.

I started by pairing the fonts alphabetically and using Fontlab's "Blend Fonts" feature to mix the pairs. This created fifteen new fonts that were crossbred again to create seven new fonts. These were distilled down to a set of four fonts, which boiled down to two, then those were blended to create one font that is the distillation of all thirty.

Despite my desire to do so, the font was not cleaned up at all along the way. On occasion, the postscript would become garbled due to incongruous letterforms — particularly the "R" and the "A" glyphs. I would average these again and, if necessary, connect a stray vector. This was the only helping hand I added to the process.

It doesn't seem that much was discovered along the way, beyond the collective adherence to the basic form of the Western alphabet. The outcome is something I feel pretty critical of — it's not a "real" typeface. It's the outcome of an experiment, that's it. Even if it were redrawn cleanly, it would be a mushy typeface. The world has enough mediocre fonts without a purpose. I find far more inspiration in legible fonts with a purpose such as Keith Tam's Arrival family.

It turned out that the greatest surprises that came from interpolation were the random bits made by more formally varying glyphs like asterisks being crossed and winding up with some neat little scraps. These were thrown together into the second spread — a sampling of the postscript-happy accidents that came out of this random process.

— Ian Lynam

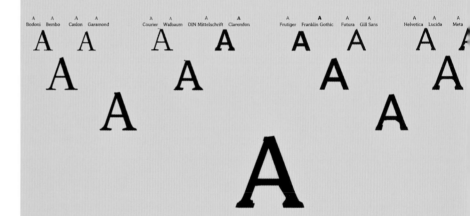

Bodoni Bembo Caslon Garamond　　Courier Walbaum DIN Mittelschrift Clarendon　　Frutiger Franklin Gothic Futura Gill Sans　　Helvetica Lucida Meta

ABCDEFGHIJKLM
abcdefghijklm

An exercise in technology: all 30 of the typefaces covered in this book interpolated into a hybrid typeface. The result looks similar to Souvenir and Cheltenham with a touch of grunge.

inion Myriad Perpetua Sabon Stempel Schneidler Times New Roman Trade Gothic Trajan VAG Rounded Universe Avenir Akzidenz Grotesk Bell Centennial Bell Gothic

NOPQRSTUVWXYZ
nopqrstuvwxyz

While a neat little experiment at examining the underlying structure of a group
of typefaces, this is not actual type design. "Mixing or sampling is
not designing." –Fred Smeijers

Specimen of F30 characters distorted by the interpolation process arranged partially.

Contributors

HENK VAN ASSEN graduated from the Royal Academy of Fine Arts (Department of Graphic Design and Typography) in The Hague, the Netherlands, in 1989. After working several years as a graphic designer in Amsterdam, he came to the United States, where he received his MFA in 1993 from Yale University. He has since worked on and participated in many projects, generally as a creative consultant, ranging from book design to visual identities to environmental graphics systems. Clients include Harry N. Abrams Publishing, New York University, the Dutch Institute for Industrial Design, the Museum of Fine Arts in Houston, the Blanton Museum of Art, and the Yale Art Gallery. He has taught in the design program of the College of Fine Arts at the University of Texas; at the School of Visual Arts in New York; and at the University of the Arts in Philadelphia. In 1999, he was appointed Critic at Yale University School of Art and is currently Director of Undergraduate Studies. Van Assen was awarded the 1999 and 2000 AIGA 50 Best Books Award; the 2002 Boston Bookbuilders Guild Best Books Award; and the 2002 and 2003 American Association of University Presses Best Books Award. Since 2004, he has been principal of HvADesign, a small studio in Brooklyn, New York.

JOSHUA BERGER is a founder and principal of Plazm, a design firm, type foundry, and publisher of *Plazm* magazine. Berger has been recognized by design publications and award shows including the AIGA Annual Show and the Art Directors Club, as well as a recent honorary exhibition at ZGRAF 9. He has received Gold Medals at the Leipzig Bookfair for his collaboration with John C. Jay on *Soul of the Game* (Melcher Media/Workman, 1997) and at the Portland Design Festival for *XXX: The Power of Sex in Contemporary Design* (Rockport, 2003). His most recent projects include the art direction and design of *Marion Jones: Life in the Fast Lane* (Warner Books, 2004), the co-curation and design of the forthcoming book *Queer Graphics: The Untold History* with writer and musician Sarah Dougher, and the development and curation of Anti-war.us, a web project that collects anti-war graphics from the international design community for distribution to activists around the world. Berger's clients, many with Plazm, have included Nike, Lucasfilm, MTV, Jantzen Swimwear, Wieden+Kennedy, J. Walter Thompson, TBWA/Chiat Day, and the Portland Institute for Contemporary Art, among others. Plazm has been named by *ID* magazine as one of the forty most influential design firms in the world and has received the Creative Resistance Award from *Adbusters*. The complete catalog of *Plazm* magazine resides in the permanent collection at the San Francisco Museum of Modern Art.

CYRUS HIGHSMITH graduated with honors from Rhode Island School of Design in 1997 and joined the Font Bureau, a digital type foundry in Boston. As senior designer there, he concentrates on the development of new type series. Highsmith is also a faculty member at RISD, where he teaches typography in the department of graphic design; in addition, he lectures and gives workshops across the United States, Mexico, and Europe. In 2001, Highsmith was featured in *Print Magazine*'s "New Visual Artist Review." His typefaces Prensa and Relay were among the winners at Bukva:Raz!, the international type design competition. He has exhibited his work in the United States and Europe. *Martha Stewart Living*, *The Source*, *Men's Health*, the Spanish edition of *Playboy*, *Rolling Stone*, the *Montreal Gazette* (Canada), and the *Sunday Independent* (London) have featured his faces. He has designed types for *La Prensa Gráfica* (El Salvador) and *El Universal* (Mexico City). In 2002 he produced a new headline series for the *Wall Street Journal* that satisfied complex contemporary requirements while remaining within the traditional typographic character that distinguishes the *Journal*.

SIMON JOHNSTON has taught typography and design at Art Center College of Design in Pasadena, California, since moving to Los Angeles from London in 1989. He is currently coordinator of typographic education in their graphic design degree program. Born in Leamington Spa, England, in 1959, he received a BA in graphic design from Bath Academy of Art, after which he studied in Switzerland at the School for Applied Arts in Basel, where his teachers included Wolfgang Weingart and Armin Hoffman. In 1984, after returning to England, he formed the design studio 8vo in partnership with Mark Holt, and in 1986 they published the first issue of *Octavo* — a journal of typography that aimed to engender fresh discussion about typography in design and the arts. 8vo worked on a wide range of projects for clients including the Institute for Contemporary Arts, Serpentine Gallery, and Factory Records. In 1989, Johnston opened his design studio, Praxis, in Los Angeles. His clients have included the Getty Trust, Los Angeles County Museum of Art, Los Angeles Contemporary Exhibitions, the University of Southern California, Princeton Architectural Press, and Virgin Records. Currently the studio specializes in publication work, particularly books. Johnston's work has earned numerous awards and has been featured in many publications, including *Cutting Edge Typography* (Rotovision, 1994) and *Making and Breaking the Grid* (Rockport, 2003).

AKIRA KOBAYASHI studied at the Musashino Art University in Tokyo, later taking a calligraphy course at the London College of Printing. Since May 2001 he has been the type director at Linotype Library GmbH. Kobayashi has recently completed the Optima Nova type family in close collaboration with the font's original designer, Hermann Zapf. He has won Best of Category and Best of Show in the 1998 *U&lc* magazine type design competition for the Clifford typeface, and first prize in the text category of Linotype Library's Third International Digital Type Design Contest for the Conrad typeface.

IAN LYNAM is a freelance designer and art director living in Tokyo, Japan.

STANLEY MOSS's career as a global brand specialist spans over forty years. He has lived and worked in locales from Southern California to New York City to Portland, Oregon (not to mention Paris, London, and Hong Kong). His experience in branding for international business encompasses assignments for clients as diverse as Citibank's International Banking Group, Coca-Cola of Belgium, the French-American Chamber of Commerce, Drexel Burnham Lambert, the *New York Times* Company, the American Hotel & Motel Association, and the University of California at Berkeley. From 1997 to 2000 Moss served as director of marketing and branding as well as chief strategist for Plazm Media, a leading design firm in the Pacific Northwest. In 2001 Moss founded Diganzi International Brand Consultancy as an interdisciplinary practice, working in conjunction with a network of specialist firms to solve higher issues of brand for international business. In August 2003, Moss was inducted into the Medinge Group, a high-level international think tank on branding headquartered in Stockholm, Sweden.

IMIN PAO is the cofounder (with Ivee Hu) of Pao & Paws, an award-winning creative agency based in Taipei, Tokyo, New York, and London. Since its inception in 1998, Pao & Paws has created commercial work for Citibank, MTV, Sony, Nike, and Levi's, among others. The firm's work has won more than forty international awards and has appeared in publications across the globe. PPbook, the publishing branch of Pao & Paws, has been producing quality creative, art, and design books since 2002. Titles include *Tomato, If You Like*, about a workshop held by the British creative group Tomato; *Dumb Luck: The Idiotic Genius of Gary Baseman*, a complete collection of the artist's work over the past ten years; and, most recently, *Clin d'Oeil*, an introduction to fifty of the most influential illustrators working today — their inspirations, thoughts, and works — and a consideration of how their work has set new standards in the world of illustration.

WOLFGANG WEINGART was born in 1941. He completed his typesetting apprenticeship in hand composition in 1963. He has taught typography at Basel School of Design since 1968 and, at the invitation of Armin Hofmann, was an instructor at the Yale Summer Program in Graphic Design in Brissago, Switzerland, from 1974 through 1996. For the last thirty years Weingart has lectured and taught extensively in Europe, North and South America, Asia, Australia, and New Zealand. His work is represented in the permanent collections of museums and private galleries and has received design awards from the Swiss Federal Department of Home Affairs in Bern. Internationally exhibited, Weingart's publications and posters have been reproduced in numerous design references and journals. He was a member of Alliance Graphique Internationale/AGI from 1978 to 1999, served on the editorial board of *Typographische Monatsblatter* fron 1970 to 1988, and contributed over twenty supplements for the educational series Typographic Process and TM/communication. A self-taught designer who fosters imagination and insight, Weingart teaches his students to teach themselves. His experimental work in typography has influenced the course of design history in the last decades of the twentieth century.

Directory

Henrik Kubel, Scott Williams
A2 Graphics
Unit G3, 35-40 Charlotte Road
London EC2A 3PG
UK
020 7739 4249
info@a2-graphics.co.uk

Michael Byzewski, Dan Ibarra
Aesthetic Apparatus
27 North 4th Street, #301
Minneapolis MN 55401
USA
612 339 3345
michael@aestheticapparatus.com

Ármann Agnarsson
Berthorugater 2
101 Reykjavik
Iceland
+354 6986959
ami@this.is
this.is/ami

Don Clark
Asterik Studio, Inc.
3524 W Government Way
Seattle WA 98199
USA
206 352 3746
don@asterikstudio.com
asterikstudio.com

Jürgen Bauer
Automat
1050 - Vienna
Ramperstorffergasse 41/6
Austria
43 1 712 22 67
automat.at
pro@automat.at

Charles Wilkin
Automatic and Design
63 Devoe Street, #2
Brooklyn NY 11211
USA
212 226 5422
info@automatic-iam.com

Andreu Balius
Milá I Fontanal 14-26, 2o2a
08012 Barcelona
Spain
34 93 459 16 52
mail@andreubalius.com

Base
158 Lafayette Street, 5th Floor
New York NY 10013
USA
212 625 9293
basenyc@basedesign.com
basedesign.com

Pere Alvaro, Àlex Gifreu
Bis]
Gran via de les Corts Cathanos,
646 5e3a, 08007 Barcelona
Spain
+34 972 674 333
bis@bisdixit.com
bisdixit.com

Michael C. Place
Build
73 Clapham Common North Side
Clapham London SW4 95B
UK
+44 7974 348494
informyou@designbybuild.com

Art Chantry
Art Chantry Design Co.
PO Box 63275
St Louis, MO 63163
USA
314 773 9421

Margo Chase
Chase Design Group
2255 Bancroft Avenue
Los Angeles CA 90039
USA
323 668 1055
margo@chasedesigngroup.com
chasedesigngroup.com

Karen Cheng
Cheng Design
2433 East Aloha Street
Seattle WA 98112
USA
206 328 4047
karencheng@comcast.net

Jim Cooper, Steve Meades
Citrus
49 Cromwell Road
Great Glen, Leicester
UK
44 870 124 8787
us@citrus.co.uk

Todd Houlette
Defacto Industries
5560 SE Ankeny Street
Portland OR 97215
USA
503 230 0289
todd@defactoindustries.com
defactoindustries.com

Takahiro Kurashima
Dentsu, Inc.
1-8-1, Higashi-shimbashi
Minato-ku, Tokyo 105-7001
Japan
03 6216 8267
takahiro.kurashima@dentsu.co.jp
dentsu.co.jp

Majid Abbasi
Did Graphics Inc.
10 Palizi Avenue
Tehran 1557974611
Iran
98 (21) 875 0217
art-director@didgraphics.com

Stephen Doyle
Doyle Partners
1123 Broadway, Suite 600
New York NY 10010
USA
212 463 8787
doylepartners.com

Emery Frost
The Gymnasium, Kings Way Place
London EC1R 0LU
UK
020 7490 7994
info@frostdesign.co.uk
emeryfrost.com

Marie Bertholle, Éric Gaspar
Éric and Marie
45, Avenue Montaigne
75008 Paris
France
+33 1 47 23 51 27
info@ericandmarie.com
ericandmarie.com

Todd Hart, Duane King
Focus2
824 Exposition, Suite 2
Dallas TX 75226
USA
214 741 4007
duane@focus2.com
focus2.com

Daniel Eatock
Foundation 33
159-173 St John Street, 4th Floor
London EC1V 4RS
UK
07903 869 248
dan@foundation33.com

Paul West
Form
47 Tabernacle Street
London EC2A 4AA
UK
44 20 4 7014 1430
paul@form.uk.com

Chris Ashworth
Creative Director
Getty Images
601 North 34th Street
Seattle WA 98103
USA
chris.ashworth@gettyimages.com

Daniel Koh
Green House
13B Bukit Pasoh Road
Singapore 089927
+65 6222 0068
daniel@greenhousedc.com

Gregg Bernstein
Hydrafuse
706 369 7161
info@hydrafuse.com

Frieda Luczak
Icon, Communications Design
Meulheimer Freiheit 125b
51063 Cologne
Germany
frieda@icon-design.de
icon-design.de

Oliver A. Krimmel,
Anja Osterwalder
i_d buero
Bismarckstrasse 67a
70197 Stuttgart
Germany
+49 (0)711 6368000
mail@i-dbuero.de
i-dbuero.de

Nathalie Barusta
Io
Föreningsgatan 6
411 27 Gothenburg
Sweden
+46 31 132947
nathalie@iodesign.nu
iodesign.nu

Kei Miyazaki
KMD
Arai 2-30-7, Nakano-ku
Tokyo 165-0026
Japan
81 3 5343 7032
kei@plants-associates.com

Sonia Diaz, Gabriel Martinez
LSD
San Andrés 36, 2o p6
28004 Madrid
Spain
lsdscape.com

Thomas Castro
LUST
Dunne Bierkade 17
2512 BC The Hague
Netherlands
+31 (0)70 3635776
tc@lust.nl
lust.nl

Ian Lynam
Tokyo, Japan
ian@ianlynam.com

Rebeca Méndez RMCD
Rebeca Méndez
Communication Design
2873 North Mount Curve Avenue
Altadena CA 91001
USA
626 794 1334
balam@earthlink.net

Mark Minelli
Minelli Inc.
381 Congress
Boston MA 02210
USA
617 426 5343
srowe@minelli.com

Paul Sahre
Office of Paul Sahre
536 Sixth Avenue, 3rd Floor
New York NY 10011
USA
212 741 7739
paul@officeofps.com
officeofps.com

Scott Stowell
Open
180 Varick Street, Room 822
New York NY 10014
USA
212 645 5633
scott@notclosed.com
notclosed.com

Garth Walker
Orange Juice Design
461 Berea Road Durban
4001 South Africa
27 31 2771860
garth@oj.co.za
oj.co.za

Imin Pao
Pao & Paws
6F, No.102, Section 2
An-ho Road, Taipei 106
Taiwan
886 2 2707 3488
info@paopaws.com
paopaws.com

Gregory Paone
Paone Design Associates LTD
242 South 20th Street, 3rd Floor
Philadelphia PA 19103
USA
215 893 0144
paonedesign@aol.com

Angus Hyland
Pentagram
11 Needham Road
London W11 2RP
UK
info@pentagram.com
pentagram.co.uk

Paula Scher
Pentagram
204 Fifth Avenue
New York NY 10010
USA
info@pentagram.com
pentagram.com

Kari Piippo
Kari Piippo Oy
Katajamäenkatu 14
FIN-50170 Mikkeli
Finland
358 15 162 187
kari@piippo.com
piippo.com

Joshua Berger
Plazm
PO Box 2863
Portland OR 97208
USA
503 528 8000
josh@plazm.com

Sabine Reinhardt
reinhardt (typo)grafisch ontwerp
Zeeburgerdijk 55
1094 AA Amsterdam
Netherlands
31 20 665 79 44
reinhardt@xs4all.nl

Stefan Sagmeister
Sagmeister Inc.
222 West 14th Street, #15
New York NY 10011
USA
info@sagmeister.com
sagmeister.com

Ralph Schraivogel
Lindenbachstr. 6
8006 Zürich
Switzerland
41 1363 23 66

Anne Shackman
Anne Shackman Design
1880 Century Park East, # 700
Los Angeles CA 90067
USA
310 279 5991
shacko@earthlink.net

Anri Seki
Sharp Communications, Inc.
425 Madison Avenue, 8th Floor
New York NY 10017
USA
212 829 0002
as@sharpthink.com
sharpthink.com

Jason Munn
The Small Stakes
377 Orange Street
Oakland CA 94610
USA
510 891 8625
jason@thesmallstakes.com

Paul Driver
Social
35 Britannia Row
Islington, London
N1 8QH
UK
+44 207 354 4422
socialuk.com

Lanny Sommese
Sommese Design
100 Rose Drive
Port Matilda PA 16870
USA
814 353 1951
lxs14@psu.edu

Steven Gilmore
SRG Design
2817 West Silver Lake Drive
Los Angeles CA 90039
USA
323 903 9488
info@srgdesaign.com

Thonik®
Weesperzijde 79d
1091 EJ Amsterdam
Netherlands
+31 (0)20 4683525
studio@thonik.nl

Clare Ultimo
Clare Ultimo Inc.
32 Union Square East, Suite 1211
New York NY 10003
USA
212 777 6973
email@clareultimo.com

Hans Bockting
UNA (Amsterdam) Designers
Korte Papaverweg 7a
1032 KA Amsterdam
Netherlands
+31 20 668 62 16
hansbockting@unadesigners.nl
unadesigners.nl

Rodrigo Sánchez
Unidad Editorial S.A.
Hermosilla, 77
28001 Madrid
Spain
34 915864776
rodrigo.sanchez@elmundo.es

Nino Brisindi
Vespina
Via del Plebiscito, 112
00186 Rome
Italy
+39 6 695251
brisindi@vespina.com
vespina.com

Andrew Blauvelt
Walker Art Center
725 Vineland Place
Minneapolis MN 55403
USA
601 375 7687
andrew.blauvelt@walkerart.org

Why Not Associates
22C Shepherdess Walk
London N17LB
UK
207 2253 2244
info@whynotassociates.com
whynotassociates.com

Todd Waterbury
Wieden+Kennedy
150 Varick Street, 7th Floor
New York NY 10013
USA
917 661 5258
todd.waterbury@wk.com
wk.com

Shawn Wolfe
Shawn Wolfe Studio
9411 17th Avenue NE
Seattle WA 98115
USA
206 322 4298
shawnwolfe@shawnwolfe.com
shawnwolfe.com

Scott Santoro
Worksight
46 Great Jones Street
New York NY 10012
USA
212 777 3558
scott@worksight.com

Mark Randall
Worldstudio
200 Varick Street, #507
New York NY 10014
USA
212 366 1317
mrandall@worldstudioinc.com